JESUS · THE · IMAGINATION

A JOURNAL OF
SPIRITUAL REVOLUTION

VOLUME ONE
2017

Angelico Press

Published by
ANGELICO PRESS

Edited by
Michael Martin

Typesetting & Design by
James R. Wetmore

Send inquiries to:
Editorial Office
8780 Moeckel Road,
Grass Lake, MI 49240
USA
mmartin@marygrove.edu
734-445-7327

ISBN 978-1-62138-282-9 pb
ISBN 978-1-62138-283-6 ebook

Front Cover:
Emi Shigeno, *Portrait of a Poet*
acrylic, finger painting and fine brush

Back Cover & Title Lettering:
Laura Hennig Cabral, *Ainsi Mon Ame*
pen on paper

Cover Design: Michael Schrauzer

CONTENTS

The Invisible

Michael Martin

WORLD contaminated by corporate greed, the abject superficiality of social media celebrity, and the commodification of the self has not left art unpoisoned. Indeed, the arts have been co-opted by all of these. Rare is the art collector today who cultivates a collection the way one might a garden—with love and eyes opened to astonishment. Instead, art is seen as an investment. Even poetry, through the proliferation of MFA programs in creative writing, which the late Franz Wright so rightly vilified with prophetic rage, has been poisoned by the marketing of the self and the snobbish camaraderie of the academic egregore. Art is now just another product and the self a brand. Our invisible tragedy.

Yet it is precisely the invisible, though another kind of invisible, that is our concern here.

Sri Aurobindo, the Indian philosopher and poet, was adamant about the prophetic role of the arts. Writing in the second decade of the twentieth century, he argued that "all art worth the name must go beyond the visible, must reveal, must show us something that is hidden, and in its total effect not reproduce but create."[1] William Blake, preceding Aurobindo by more than two-hundred years, articulated a position even more pointed: "Let every Christian as much as in him lies engage himself openly & publicly before all the World in some Mental pursuit for the Building up of Jerusalem."[2] Is there any other way to be a Christian? I think not.

Art has the potential to create a new Gospel every day. Not a different one, but a new one, and this through the incarnational possible. I have always felt extreme irritation at the dismissal of imagination from poetry first proposed by John Ruskin with his notion of "the pathetic fallacy" that was perfected by the New Critics, internalized by Poststructuralism, and then turned into a kind of religion by the proponents of an amateurish Deconstruction that must have annoyed Jacques Derrida, one of the great negative theologians, to no end. The pathetic fallacy is neither. As Kathleen Raine has written, "It is not 'the words on the page' which create the god in question, but the reverse."[3] Most contemporary critics, however, would

---

[1] Sri Aurobindo, *The Future Poetry with 'On Quantitative Metre'* (Pondicherry: Sri Aurobindo Ashram, 1997), 8.
[2] William Blake, *Jerusalem*, plate 77.
[3] Kathleen Raine, *Defending Ancient Springs* (West Stockbridge, MA: Inner Traditions / Lindisfarne Press, 1985), 118.

suggest that anyone proposing such an idea "be used for making atonement by sending him into the wilderness."[4] Sometimes only blood satisfies.

JESUS THE IMAGINATION was conceived on the Feast of St. Mary Magdalen, 2016, during a conversation at Stella Matutina Farm in Grass Lake, Michigan, with temperatures sweltering to ninety-seven degrees. That evening we chanted Divine Liturgy in the barn, broke bread, and swam beneath the stars in the darkness of the pond. Some of the participants of that conference are represented in these pages, some were present in spirit, and some were somehow awakened to the impulse by methods quite beyond my knowing.

Our intention was then, and is now, not altogether modest: the regeneration of Christian art and culture. But we believe such is possible only by grounding this regeneration in the primordial regeneration of the earth and all it contains that began at Golgotha: for without this there is no regeneration, only repetition and dissipation. This regeneration is always already happening; it calls us into the future and cautions us to resist retreating into the past. For backwards is the way of the fearful: St. Peter almost drowned following that approach. The Lord bids us walk with him on the sea. The call to regeneration, furthermore, is inherently parousaic. As Guillaume Apollinaire so accurately describes it, *"que seuls le renouvellent ceux qui sont fondés en poésie"*—only those will remake the world who are rooted in poetry.

Dare to see the heavenly country, brothers and sisters.

EASTERTIDE, 2017

4 Leviticus 16:10.

BLOOD　　　　　　*SPIRIT*　　　　　　*FLESH*

Saturn Return, Matthew Livermore, linocut

REVERBERATION

Ruth Asch

Hear this voice die.
A blue arabesque in the mind,
last cry of a distant figure
you will be too late to save—
on the edge, arms outstretched like a bird,
cast to the mindless void
and a deathless grave.

Why should you struggle or sigh
for child-bearing maid, supplicant priest,
preacher or prophet hard-spoken,
the mourner at a feast?

This is a Christian farewell,
song in the key of hunted swan.
The murmur of these words
spills ghostly tears in the floods of Babylon.

Yurodivy

Therese Schroeder-Sheker

For Bernard McGinn, in great gratitude

FUNDAMENTAL teaching embodied in Russian Orthodox mysticism concerns the path of the *yuro-divy.* Against all odds, the *yurodivy* or holy fool of Christ voluntarily suffers affliction yet does so with the kind of meaning, purpose, and intention that becomes fruitful. This kind of folly does not point to neurotic[1] or fruitless suffering, but the opposite. Sacred folly becomes fruit-bearing because, however confusing or paradoxical, its suffering engenders a condition of complete simplicity, costing not less than everything.[2]

I lay down my life in order to take it up
   again.
No one takes it from me, but I lay it
   down on my own.
I have power to lay it down, and power
   to take it up again.
                    (John 10:17–18)

The voluntary suffering of the holy fool appears or emerges following years or decades of preparatory formation. This includes prayer, meditation, contemplation, worship, a sacramental life, observance of and participation in the liturgical year *and* the seasons in nature, and a deeply embodied sacralization of time. During the preparatory years, one has inadvertently become tempered, not unlike the process required to create a superior tuning fork. When the alloyed metal of the tuning fork is exposed to rhythmically alternating periods of heat and cold, the matter at hand becomes an instrument. The tuning fork gradually becomes tensile enough to be able to hold two conditions simultaneously: precise attunement to form and unusually subtle, immediate responsivity. By extension, the holy fool becomes an instrument and instrumental as a shaping force, whether or not understood or appreciated.

For the *yurodivy*, this tempering process can happen amidst all of life's routines, choices, and responsibilities rather than as a result of something exotic. One can become tempered through faithfulness amidst life's ordinary events and daily pressures. During the course of this "ordinary" development, slowly but surely, virtues become part of one's faithfulness. They become a way of being and rip-

---

[1] Helen Luke (1904–1995). See her chapter on suffering in *Old Age: Journey into Simplicity* (Lindisfarne, 2010).
[2] T.S. Eliot (1888–1965). See "Little Gidding" from his *Four Quartets* (New York: Harcourt, 1943).

ple out into larger circles of life, not unlike overtones in music. There is no Cecile B. DeMille fanfare accompanying the emergence of virtue. A man or woman may be humble or generous, truthful or patient, loving or forgiving. He or she becomes so to a very pure degree; the most virtuous footprint is usually invisible.

In the crucial moments when one most authentically *serves* generosity or patience, truth or kindness, love or forgiveness, attention is not drawn to self. The servant disappears. Although it will later be needed, courage is the farthest thing from the *yurodivy's* capacity or mind. Yet, unknowingly, the human-making curriculum shall have had a summative impact. The "unnamed" novitiate of ordinary life and growing virtue gradually midwifes a new man or a new woman. The human being is transformed, and does not yet know it, but those virtues are going to congeal soon, like water in a reservoir. From that reservoir, one is going to find the private courage to silently know and live the Pauline "*Not I, but the Christ in me*," and the Johannine and Marian grammar of assent, "*Yes*." To make matters more complicated, the holy fool does not always appear in the same form through time and culture, but still walks a particular vocation.

In one picture of the *yurodivy*, life is happening in an ordinary way. A man or woman may be doing what they do every day, every season. Yet something baleful happens. The sudden spark of a destructive mechanism called psychological projection erupts and colors the surrounding terrain. That gentle person, that quiet person—or especially the one who has

been transparent—shows up in the middle of the field, and thus the drama unfolds. An individual who is projecting throws his or her own contents onto a light-filled screen, seeing in another what they fail to see in themselves. Through absence of reflection, and through lack of self-knowledge, a person or a collective may attempt to avoid personal responsibility for the things most ailing them. In this way, from out of a blue, a *yurodivy* can become a target or a scapegoat for the unacknowledged shadow material of others, or for the projections of an agitated group. The undigested, habituated, unconscious matter (such as resentment, anger, fear, shame, blame, cynicism, disappointment, jealousy) can accumulate and fester within the hearts or minds of even a few—two or three is all it takes. But those few can successfully incite something destructive in others, to the degree that the others remain unreflective. A little gossip begins and spreads like wildfire. In contemporary terms, the strategic circulation of misinformation or disinformation can result in psychic, physical, and cultural violence.

In addition to the New Testament, mythopoetic images, traditional stories, and remarkable books and films portray very sensitive, symbolic teachings about how or why projection happens. (Orpheus being dismembered by the spears of the frenzied Maenads;[3]

---

[3] See Therese Schroeder-Sheker, "Orpheus and the Eternal: Faithfulness and Fine-Tuning," in the *Zoe* 1, Nos. 5 & 6 (September 2004). In the Orpheus legend, the Maenads cannot and do not hear or listen to or respond

the Irish, English, or Scottish sin eater; *Brother of Sleep*[4] or *Andrei Rublev*.[5]) If we can *be with* this kind of traditional material, learn from it, be present to it—in Michael Martin's agapeic way[6]—there is much to be gleaned. The drama of psychological projection and the scapegoating process have a great deal to teach the Faithful, including the Faithful Remnant within the Christian community and far beyond her borders—to all our brothers and sisters across miles and identities. If the viewer or reader can begin to see how the bits and fragments of personal and self-serving deception or wrath start to spill out and circulate in expressions of psychic, cultural, or physical violence, we begin to draw near to the heart of the *metanoic, kenotic* transformation to which all Johannine spirituality leads. Let us return for another moment to the archetype of the Holy Fool.

Who is targeted when these projective spears fly? The king or the mayor?

No. The town pauper, the woodcutter, the quiet weaver, the midwife living at the edge of the forest, the one who has been born mute or might have a paralyzed hand or clubbed foot. In ordinary life, most adults are whole enough and secure enough to know and to acknowledge their imperfections, their sins, their shortcomings; and the holy fool has no problem sincerely admitting imperfection on any level because of this normal (not exceptional) maturity. But now the attack begins and a fury is unleashed. The *yurodivy* weaver or *yurodivy* woodcutter is suddenly blamed for the collective's ills and disappointments. The mob says that it is *that one's* fault that the well is dry, the cattle die, the child is blind, a draught decimates the fields or orchards, husbands or wives stray, and the taxes are painful. When the mob attacks, the *yurodivy* is reviled, scorned, hated, or abused. He or she might be dragged, spat upon, beaten, or stoned. In one way or another, the *yurodivy* is held hostage by an aberration of justice. Here is the theological and spiritual essential: the *yurodivy* does not return violence or hatred with reaction or with reactive violence. This doesn't mean that he or she doesn't suffer. It means that in making a conscious choice, in remaining disarmed, the *yurodivy* remains more deeply anchored in the memory of the suffering endured by Christ. I do not mean to fast-forward, but the Epistle of James recognizes certain fire trials as initiatory processes, and, without being dismissive of suffering, tells us to *consider the affliction in joy*. When used as a diagnostic, the later joy emerges as part of the economy of redemptive transformation.

to words or his voice. They become possessed of frenzied hatred, a cocktail of anger and pride, because he has declined their advance or proposal. They decide to kill him, and with elemental fury swarm him with spears, in this case, symbolic of the penetrating quality of anger or fury. But Orpheus holds out his hands in supplication. He remains unarmed, disarmed though he is dismembered. Later, he becomes a star in the sky

[4] See the difficult, little understood, but remarkable 1996 Joseph Vilsmaier film *Brother of Sleep*, from the Robert Schneider book of the same title. In this work, one sees two kinds of *yurodivy* framed within a story about a gentle and unusually pure musical genius and his experience of the harmony of the spheres.

[5] See the 1966 film of the same name, directed by Andrei Tarkovsky.

[6] See his *The Incarnation of the Poetic Word* (2017).

At the deepest level, the life-work of the *yurodivy* sustains an initiation process that does not speak of evil from a safe distance, nor from abstraction or theory, history or analysis. Like a compass pointing true north, the *yurodivy* orientation actually encounters and witnesses evil. The *yurodivy* learns to know evil from within and does this by shared or participatory suffering. The spiritual elders describe how the *yurodivy* actually comes to know and understand evil from the inside, meets the contagion or the destructive content through suffering *by intimacy with* rather than *avoidance of* and, in many cases, attains *kardiognosis*—seeing into the heart of another, even from a distance. However anguished an initial entry into the experience of a collective maw may be or has been, the *yurodivy* realizes that he or she will not be overcome by the poison of the diabolical deception or the cunning injustice *if* a genuine Encounter occurs. *If* is the key word. *If* a genuine Encounter occurs, understanding does, too, and the role of compassion later becomes palpable.

I have come to understand that the Encounter lived in sacred folly is triadic, not dual. The holy fool encounters the mob or the vengeful accuser, and also makes room for (remains open to, invites, waits for) the presence of the Unknown Third: the spiritual world. The presence of a spiritual being is experienced,[7] whether an angel, a saint, one of the Evangelists, Mary, Christ. Yes, even *today*.

Encounter (meeting-knowing-understanding) then leads to the ability to transfigure the evil, the injustice, the deception, the malady; and in so doing, however invisibly, the scorned and reviled fool who has been held hostage or incarcerated (or even killed) eventually becomes the source of a greater medicine or a cultural vaccination process. Think of Francis foolishly giving away his beautiful clothes, marrying Lady Poverty, and washing lepers. A few of the members of the Franciscan community scorned him, but he was visited by no less than a seraphim.

Not to be confused with operatic romanticism, an evil voluntarily shouldered in sustained affliction most definitely entails anguish; and yet (not unlike the best tuning fork) through repeated tempering the initial shock is replaced with quiet, centered, anchored, and persevering focus.[8] The voluntary suffering generates new capacities, among them: patience, an embodied, ensouled understanding, a different kind of compassion, a purified love. By voluntarily taking in the evil *directly through the region of the heart*, for the sake of others—resulting in a communion with affliction itself—the *yurodivy* gradually transfigures an evil action or trend. He or she comes to know an evil intimately, and does not deny it, does not surgically remove it, and does not leave the detritus for others to clean up. Not entirely unlike the Irish or traditional sin eater, but entirely close to the heartbeat of Christ, the *yurodivy* absorbs and transforms.

---

[7] Our friends in interreligious dialogue remind us that in Buddhism one may also be surrounded and aided by spiritual beings from multiple levels.

[8] The etymology of the Latin *focus* and hearth being the same, and including warmth or fire.

In light of the fact that it is widely proclaimed that we are alive in a post-modern, post-Christian, and post-truth era, the witness of a contemporary *yurodivy* named Iulia de Beausobre[9] (23 October 1893–20 December 1977) offers much insight. Her rose-gold gem "Creative Suffering" reflects upon one of the most poignant, but perhaps overlooked, details in the mystical literature. She also offers a contemporary application of the spiritual practice of *metanoia*.

Iulia had been incarcerated in the Lubyanka Prison in 1932, and her husband and infant son died during the same period. Rather than recount lurid details of the specific ways in which she had been tortured by five sadistic jailors, she describes instead the simultaneity of both terror and serenity. She describes survival, not through numbness, nor passivity, but through heightened consciousness and presence of being, regardless of the intensity of the torture. She describes how she had to learn how to remain present to what was happening. This allowed her to go all the way through it, not around it, by intimacy with Christ. She also recounts a variation on a crucial heroic legend, and describes how this gave her (and other prisoners at Lubyanka) healing fortitude and life.

The legend speaks of "the great Russian battle against one-eyed Falsehood." George the Valiant is fighting the Adversary, but is suddenly struck off his horse by an enormous power.

In a reversal of heartbreaking poignancy, Christ Himself *shields* Falsehood for a period, until the Archangel Michael arrives. Michael succeeds in combat and slays the dragon, whereas George did not. Later, Christ explains to George that he had not been worthy to slay Falsehood because *his knowledge of evil had been too limited!* "Only those who have themselves drained every drop of the cup of evil may, after their regeneration, shatter it without fear of bringing woe upon themselves or upon the world." Understanding transfigures; avoidance, denial, surgical removal, and projection do not—they lengthen and elongate pain, rather than redeem. Later, Iulia recounts: *"The inability to suffer sometimes proves to be the greatest evil of all."* The path of holy folly shines a bright light, as does she.

It seems clear that the internet has deftly facilitated and enabled the exponential proliferation of good *and* evil uses of:

Word, Memory, and Narrative

In the days and years to come, we will need to see modern fictions and expressions of scapegoating and projection for what they truly are. Let us look deep within, return to Iulia de Beausobre's legacy, and remember the vocation of the *yurodivy*. The disarmed and holy fool walks a much needed lightning path. May we hear its thunder, and pray for strength.

*The Chalice of Repose Project
On the anniversary of the transitus
of St. Seraphim of Sarov*

[9] See Iulia de Beausobre, *Creative Suffering* (Convent of the Incarnation/Fairacres Oxford: SLG Press). This author is also known under her second name: Lady Julia Namier.

THREE POEMS

Katie Hartsock

CHILD WITH DROID

There's a heartbeat in you
whose mother blow-dries her hair
by the stalls while you sit
a white towel spread
between the locker room bench
and your nakedness perfectly
cloaked by your posture

    As in a masterful painting
    masterful centuries ago
    a *putto* but a girl
    this time and holding the phone
    she gave to divert
    you who cannot use it

        Staring it down absolutely intent
        you are un-interruptable
        as *Boy with Thorn* the sculpture
        I photographed with a disposable
        camera how belovable
        his concentration on
        plucking that spine from his foot

    And so the familiar impulse of mine
    to pick you up is halted
    not by the familiar prohibition—
    Katie you cannot just
    pick up other people's children—
    but rather as by the museum signs
    I kept reading one summer
    Berühren verboten   Non
    toccare   an outstretched
    hand in a red circle
    with a red line through it

You pay as little mind
as that boy beautiful of course
beautifully hunched over
in absorption like yours
and reproduced so many times
from Hellenistic fountains
to the Esquiline hill
to Medici gardens—even
Napoleon confiscated a copy
—and Brunelleschi when tasked
with *The Sacrifice of Isaac*
gave one of the servants
who abide with the ass
at the bottom of the mountain this very
position of distraction

>He never looks up to check
>what manner of worship works
>his master
>but only attends
>to that thorn in his arch
>—Lo Spinario of Moriah

>>Someone set that Genesis scene
>>for the open
>>competition to ornament
>>the Florentine baptistery
>>so parents coming through the doors
>>with babes in arms would see
>>—*See how closely loss remains*
>>*a possible necessity*
>>—*See all your tests reflected here*
>>—*See what you are given freely*

>Brunelleschi's piece
>took second place
>and was not used   it is thought
>he paid too much attention
>to the servant's bodies
>—See what I can do with them, too—
>it diverted the eye
>from the main quatrefoil
>the knife the angel the halted arm

Here I am says Abraham
Your mother is coming
her hair is dry but you
still stare at the blank dark screen
you cannot dig it out

      You had been swimming
      The both of you
      in the pool
      I'm preparing to get in

            You know what Catherine
            of Siena said about swimming—
            he who dives into the sea
            and swims under the water
            sees nothing but ocean and what
            has sunk beneath it

      He cannot perceive
      anything outside those waters
      they demand all

Your attention every blood pulse
which we were ready completely
to give but she wasn't
really talking about swimming

PLANNING OUR DREAM FLORIDA VACATION

For T

In an old poem where one of the monsters vomits books,
a blazoned girl must walk alone through the forest
at night, on a deep dark deadline

to deliver a message that will save her love.
Frightened but not afraid she goes, and very certain,
in the words she prays, and

in where prayers land—and then, a lion
emerges from the jowls of the shadows
to lick her hand,

to know devotion for the first time in his lionly life, to escort her
till dawn. She pets his mane as they walk, she can see
he won't take a name.

It is like they talk all through the night
but neither will remember about what.
When you and I take our dream trip to Florida,

between Weeki Wachi and Cape Canaveral
we will face some dangers—pornocratic kings who would keep us
in the swamp forever—

but evade others by grace—circling marshy homes of monsters
who eat the unsuspecting and vomit up the internet,
we make it back to the car

unassailed and indigestible. With insulin and inhalers we maintain
our machinery, and on gas station maps we make notes.
Lions do not protect those

*who think they need protecting. Lions love place-names like Pilachua
and Milwaukee. Lions do not come to cowards or uncertain hearts
except to make them run.*

We eat shrimp and sing unicorn songs. *Lions pity the fool.*
In the territory of mermaids and astronauts, we have a message
to deliver, a love to save.

WAITING TO SEE THE SUPER BLOOD MOON ON A
CLOUDY NIGHT AT THE WATERFRONT CAFE

This pint glass is the earth,
this cell phone is the sun,
and the lip gloss moon comes here to make
a total lunar eclipse—

shoreline conversations
rehearse astronomy
and build terrestrial replicas
of celestial revolutions

we trouble to recall.
A drunk astrologist
is loudly insisting: meaning exists!
in these patterns, for the extraordinary

favors order. When the clouds
eventually part and the glazy
globe like a dimly lit red ship
appears, everyone cheers

as if we're watching our team
take the lead. An oldies station
plays The Drifters' "Under the Boardwalk,"
and I sing along although

I've never liked the chorus,
how the voices modulate
into a minor key as lovers
lay their blanket below

in damp wooden darkness, a question
we all know the answer to,
like whether the tide's going in
or out. Tell me, night,

in your alignment, how
to make the world attend
a shadow, seduced by what's concealed
and breathless to turn off

the lights. Diminished into
strips, the clouds perform
a never-ending dance of veils.
Most people start to leave.

Chicago's glimmer in
the distance seems more constant
than the moon, which made us wait
to revel in its face,

a kind of groveling
we reveled in before
our revels disappeared and we
denied we ever knelt.

TWO POEMS

R. Bratten Weiss

COUNTING COINS

We arrive at the wayside place to count our winnings,
and I find my pockets heavy with regrets.
I am rich in longing for the things I cast away,
rich in disgust for myself,
jingling coins effaced by too much handling.

Oh, but there's no use in pretending: I've hoarded them,
a miser of these oily pennies I've labored to possess,
and I like the regret, and I like the longing, and
I like the look of my hand's dry bones as I raise my glass.
I like to laugh at those whose coins are new and glittering.

And to count also the things I don't regret,
lying on my back on a the ridge above the canyon,
numbering them, forever remote, a million lives away, each worth empires:

the moment in late summer when the first geese took flight,
soaring like Icarus, but wiser than any winged child,
when the wind turned and rolled us towards the season's end, and
everything was drying, fading into gold
and I was standing in the garden, with tomato vines sharp and bronze
    around me,
and I was eating tomatoes from the vine, thinking:
tomorrow was the last time that I saw you,
tomorrow was the moment out of reach.

Here's a thing to know: no matter how long the summer, you will never
regret plucking fruits from the vine and eating, sweat on the brow, pollen
    glittering in the air,
for the wind rolls, the vines lie dead, seeds scattered like stars on the soil,
and you will find yourself alone in a wayside place
counting tarnished coins.

THE GUEST

Another summer now prepares to take her leave, all grains and grasses golden,
in her fine hat she waves to us, heading westward with the sun, a happy lady on
    a train—
the rest of us earth-bound, staid, dust on our shoes. And once again, I've failed
    to find
whatever it was I was sent for, she's forgotten once again to whisper in my ear
    the secret
that was promised, mislaid the map she meant to give me, the one with the
sketch of the box elder split by the storm, the journey of the water, the X
that marks the spot.

Or perhaps I heard wrong. I'm sure I was attentive that
Long-lost day, some July or August in the golden mists of newborn years,
    when I strode
whistling from the pine woods and saw a copperhead coiled like eternity on
    the dry grass,
fixing me with its knowing, agate eye,
or perhaps it was the suave cat perched on a gate. Something spoke when I
    expected silence,
and said to me: wait.
Just wait. Something fabulous is coming, something intricate as fretted stars
    on a jeweled crown,
as fireflies in the dusk, something joyful as running horses or clear water.

Since then, I've harvested the good and bad together, the ripe tomatoes and
    the bitter gourds,
I've seen the dry pavements drink deep of the blood of innocents, war striding,
viruses transmuting.

I've found much wonder and some shame, but I think I got the message
    wrong,
I think perhaps there was nothing I was meant to wait for, but only the spare
    moments
dropping like dew in the morning, moments for courage, or justice, or
    perhaps
only, after all, for patience, until it comes my time to speak,
shattering the new-born day
when all expected silence.

Little green men against muddy red creatures:

Postmodern Deep Ecology in Saint Exupéry's *Le Petit Prince* and the Sacramental Depth of the Earth in Pope Francis's *Laudato Si'*

Sebastián Montiel & Aaron Riches

Dedicated to Carmen, new arrival to her Father's Earth

I

IT IS UNLIKELY that Pope Francis wrote *Laudato Si'* to be read as an explicit critique of Antoine de Saint Exupéry's celebrated tale, *Le Petit Prince*. It is less likely that the relative popularity of *Laudato Si'* will displace *Le Petit Prince* as a favorite children's bedtime story. And yet the two texts are well understood together, since *Laudato Si'* is an implicit critique of *Le Petit Prince* and the vision of the being and spirit it proposes, insofar as the latter is a rereading of the Christian story of creation in light of the crisis of modernity and the secular collapse that pretends to give a new spiritual depth to a world that is now "post-Christian." And not only so: just as *Laudato Si'* is intended to become a spiritual *cri de coeur* for a Catholic ecology so *Le Petit Prince* has recently come to be invoked as something of a foundational religious text for the movement of Deep Ecology.

More than simply offering rival spiritual-ecological visions, *Laudato Si'* and *Le Petit Prince* generate their respective visions out of two essentially different acts of remembrance: the former, through a faithful act of Christian remembering that preserves and holds fast to the tradition, while the latter through an act of explicit *mis*remembering that "remembers" Christian figures and tropes only in order to break fundamentally with and undermine the Christian vision. In fact, the allegedly naïve story of *Le Petit Prince* is, we will see, more than a mere rereading of the Christian story; it is a quasi-gnostic act of *mis*remembering, after the type of Hegel's *mis*remembering of Christianity.[1] In this light *Le Petit Prince* is at once a text that is both "heretical" and "modern." Specifically, what is at stake is the liq-

---

[1] Cf. Cyril O'Regan, *The Anatomy of Misremembering: Von Balthasar's Response to Philosophical Modernity*, Vol. 1: *Hegel* (Chestnut Ridge: The Crossroad Publishing Company, 2014).

uidation of *concrete* memory, that is, memory as an act of concrete remembrance of a real history, a complex tapestry of evental and personal facts that are themselves irreducible to "principles." In a gnostic fashion, the act of *misremembering* enacted by *Le Petit Prince* gestures to some of the constitutive tropes of Christianity in a way that now subtly equivocates them, appearing to be faithful in a new guise, but in fact reconfiguring them at their basis: liquidating what is concrete and real, what is namable and historically specific, and reshaping these tropes now in the form of abstraction, principles that are constitutively nameless. And this is done to such an extent that the very concreteness on which Christian religion is based is now wholly pulverized.

At stake, first of all, is the idea of creation as a relation of an "I" with a "Thou." For *Laudato Si',* as we will see, this is basic to the whole of the Pope's proposal, while for *Le Petit Prince* it is made *a priory* unthinkable. Attendants to this are the latter's ephemeralization of eschatological hope, uprooted from concrete history (the origin and the event of Incarnation), and new hope in the progress of Spirit, and the need not so much to remember a foundation "bond" of communion, but the human project of "spirit" (or of heart) to forge new and future "bonds" of humanity. Just as Hegel's "Christian" philosophy kept some of the basic symbolism and grammar of Christian theology, but reconfigured it at the service of a new vision of the modern state and the "end of history" in the triumph of *Geist,* so *Le Petit Prince* remembers certain aspects of the Christian religion only to misre-

member the Christian story to such an extent that it is epigone. And this epigone has recently become a key sentimental and "spiritual" touchstone for modern worshippers of so-called "Deep Ecology," invented in the seventies as a reaction against the former and shallower "reformist environmentalism."[2] For adherents of this creed, *Le Petit Prince* has become a sacred text, imbuing this ecological movement with a piety and a spiritual horizon. Like Hegelianism, Deep Ecology is less concerned with concrete facts of history and real specific beings, and more concerned with processes of history and ecology, deracinated from the concrete life of any "I" that could stand before a real "Thou."

Deep Ecology gives a "religious" answer to a new species of "fear of death" provoked by recent and radical technological advances. These advances have at once given us a heightened sense of modern science and technology's power, which appears as a force unlimited, both as a power to wholly destroy the Earth (through atomic war or ecological disaster), while at the same time solve (and save) the same Earth from natural disasters and from that age old problem of "death."[3] The new fear of death is not the old fear of an individ-

[2] Arne Naess, "The Shallow and the Deep: Long-Range Ecology Movement," *Inquiry* 16 (1973): 95–100.

[3] *Journal of Evolution and Technology* 14 (2005): 1–25; Bruce J. Klein (ed), *The Scientific Conquest of Death: Essays on Infinite Lifespans* (Buenos Aires: Libros en Red, 2004); and Ronald Cole-Turner (ed), *Transhumanism and Transcendence: Christian Hope in an Age of Technological Enhancement* (Washington, DC: Georgetown University Press, 2011).

ual being, but the abstract fear of the whole of the human species (and perhaps the "planet"); it is an apocalyptic fear of a certain imminent "end of history." Beginning with a sound criticism of destructive anthropocentrism and consumerism, Deep Ecology ends by inviting us to worship a deified Earth which will redeem us through a more or less violent dissolution of all "harmful" differences: created-uncreated, alive-inert, human-nonhuman, man-woman. So, even if believers of this new creed usually come disguised as ecological sheep, the ubiquitous "biological diversity" has made these evolved Malthusian wolves to present themselves under three guises: gnostic-Manichaean, pantheist-Spinozist and agnostic-neoliberal—all of which showing their teeth both from the traditional "left" and "right" of the political spectrum.[4]

Ecologists were not the first to grasp the long philosophical scope of the famous story of the gentle little prince who fell to the Earth. Martin Heidegger once called *Le Petit Prince* "one of the great existentialist books of the century." As Heidegger rightly saw, Saint Exupéry's tale was less a little children's book than a serious response to the *magna questio* of Saint Augustine: *Where does the human being come from and where is he going?* And it is specifically in this way that

the little novella can be read as presuming a modernist and apocryphal retelling of the Judeo-Christian "beginning," the Genesis story of human origins. The suggestion here is this: if we want to see clearly the *novum* of Pope Francis's provocation, we do well contrasting it with a powerful prototype of the modern and secular vision, here for our purposes encapsulated in *Le Petit Prince*. And so: if the integral ecology of *Laudato Si'* is rooted in the unique memory of the Judeo-Christian "beginning" (and, more implicitly, "end"), the deep ecological vision of *Le Petit Prince* is rooted in an other, apocryphal, misremembering of the "beginning" (and "end"). What, then, are the characteristics of each? Let us begin with Genesis.

The narrative of Genesis knows no abstraction. Whatever the "universal" is, in Genesis it can be nothing but a concrete universal. Genesis is a narrative of particular facts brought out of the darkness of nothing. Genesis is as concrete a narrative as one could hope to find. Accordingly, the process of creation is a process of concrete invocation, of differentiation, and of naming:

> And God said, "Let there be light," and there was light. And God saw that the light was good. And God separated the light from the darkness. God called the light Day, and the darkness he called Night. And there was evening and there was morning, the first day. (Gen 1:3–5)

In this narration of the beginning of being, nothing is empty of meaning. There are no "gods," there is a God whose name is *Yhwh*. There is no

---

[4] See, for instance, M. Munakata, "Lessons from The Little Prince," *Science & Children* 42 (2005); and Q. Li and G. Hou, "From Breaking the Traditional Fairy Tale Narrative to Criticizing the Sickness of Modern Civilization: Comment on Stylistic Innovation and Ideological Connotation in The Little Prince by Exupéry," *Journal of HIT, Social Sciences Edition* (2006).

"humanity": there is the human being *Adam*. There is no ethereal "eternal feminine" symbolized by a capricious flower: there is the woman *Eve*. There are no "planets," there is the planet *Earth*. In Genesis only the snake bears a generic name. The whole frame and inner structure of being are accordingly constituted in the intimacy of meaningful and concrete relations. The Earth is Adam's home, and Adam is the creature God creates "in our image, after our likeness" (Gen 1:26). Herein the most intimate relation— the relation that lies both at the source and summit of creation—is filial: Adam is the "son of God," which is to say that God is Adam's *Father* (cf. Lk 3:38). Everything, in the Judeo-Christian vision of "genesis" is implicated in these bonds of interrelation, deriving from this most intimate and central relation of God the Father with his human son, Adam. This "original" relation, in the image and after likeness, is not chronological but analogical: the precedent is that of God the Father in relation to the eternally begotten Son, Jesus. "The Father loves the Son and has placed everything in his hands" (John 3:35). Bonds of being and interconnectedness are of the very essence of being as such, at least as it is discovered in Genesis. "Relation," thus, at once precedes being and is directly constitutive of its "substantial" fact. In time this will come to furnish the Christian doctrine of the Trinity, according to which the Persons of the Trinity are understood as "subsistent relations." The metaphysical weight of "relation" as a category

alongside as constitutive of "substance" is already felt here.[5]

Because the being of creation is constituted in relation to God, and only exists by the gift that flows from (and is) this relation, there can be no inherently destructive potentialities, and so "nothing is intrinsically evil."[6] Or, formulated according to the classical Augustinian doctrine of *privatio boni*: evil is a privation and thus, unlike the good, it is essentially unsubstantial; evil is parasitic on the goodness that *is*. A more biblical way of expressing all of this is to say that evil issues from "enmity," the refusal to see God's work as beautiful and to accept God's love as the paternal gift that sustains everything that is "in being." Hence, to be evil, in the Gospel of John, is to be the devil, the murderer and destroyer of being, who is no giver of life because in him there is "no truth" (John 8:44). The essentially counterfeiting nature of evil is here made most clear in the fact that this "father," the devil, is "the father of lies," or as the original Greek text has it *"oti pseustês estin kai o patêr autou,"* which could as easily be translated: he "is a liar and the father of *himself*" (referring *"autou"* to *"patêr"* rather than to *"pseustês"*). To be evil is to present oneself as fatherless.

The vision of "genesis" presumed in *Le Petit Prince* is precisely "fatherless." From its very basis, then, it is opposite to the Judeo-Christian Genesis as a

---

[5] Cf. Joseph Cardinal Ratzinger, *Introduction to Christianity*, trans. J.R. Foster (San Francisco:

Ignatius Press, 2004), 183: Because in Trinitarian terms, the persons of the Trinity are "subsistent relations," henceforth *"relatio . . .* stands beside . . . substance as an equally primordial form of being."

[6] Nicetas Pectoratus, *Spiritual Paradise* 3 (Sources chrétiennes, 8.64–65).

counterfeit is opposed to the truth. This is signaled in the first place by the fact that we find in the whole of *Le Petit Prince* not one single proper name. We never hear of the name of the redheaded protagonist, much less that of the "little prince," whose strange habit of avoidance of directly answering any of the narrator's questions confirms an abstracting and vague narrative of being. Over the course of the eight days the protagonist is stranded in the desert attempting to repair his plane as the little prince recounts to him the story of his life. It is a "genesis" narrative of sorts, significantly unfolded over the symbolically pregnant number of *eight* days, correspondent with the Christian days of creation and redemption. The prince describes life on his planet: a world he possesses for himself, devoid of the integral relations of being as well as the complex tapestry of evental and personal facts that we find basic to the Judeo-Christian idea of "the Earth." The prince's home-planet is more a possession to dominate than a common home to cultivate. B-612, as the protagonist assumes the prince's planet to be, is an asteroid-sized planet, on which the lone inhabitant is less a cultivator than weed-killer. The little prince describes spending his earlier days clearing unwanted seeds and sprigs of his planet, especially baobab trees, which are constantly growing to choke the surface of his asteroid. The prince's desire for a sheep was precisely for this: to eat undesirable plants.

Indeed, the agricultural and breeding strategies of the little prince do not follow at all the advice of God to Adam on care of the Earth. Saint Exupéry's would-be "green" little man is neither a Good Farmer nor a Good Shepherd. According to the narrator, in B-612,

> There were good seeds from good plants, and bad seeds from bad plants. But seeds are invisible. They sleep deep in the heart of the earth's darkness, until someone among them is seized with the desire to awaken. Then this little seed will stretch itself and begin—timidly at first—to push a charming little sprig inoffensively upward toward the sun. If it is only a sprout of radish or the sprig of a rose-bush, one would let it grow wherever it might wish. But when it is a bad plant, one must destroy it as soon as possible, the very first instant that one recognizes it.[7]

As opposed to the created Earth, which surrounds Adam and Eve as a gratuitous gift, an invitation to communion, planet B-612 is a modern Manichaean asteroid where "good" and "evil" sprout and grow independent of any relation with any "creator" (who must be either nonexistent or suppressed in Saint Exupéry's fatherless vision). Christianity has always seen that "creation is beautiful and harmonious, and God has made it all just for your sake; he has made it beautiful, grand, varied, and rich."[8] In B-612, things and relations are neither intrinsically beautiful nor good, and so neither is there any possibility of a Fall, a falling way form the truth of being in its beauty and goodness. In

[7] Antoine de Saint Exupéry, *The Little Prince* (Mammoth: London, 1943), 20–21.
[8] Saint John Chrysostom, *On Providence*, 7.2.

this dangerous soil, the only farmer must destroy bad plants "as soon as possible." And this is just the opposite manner of farming to that of the "man who sowed good seed in his field, but while his men were sleeping, his enemy came and sowed weeds among the wheat and went away" (Matt 13:24–25). That man did not belong to "the world of efficiency" (cf. LS 108–09), as both the little prince and mechanical harvesters do. He belonged to "the world of love." These two incompatible worlds, as they are described by Wendell Berry,[9] give rise to two corresponding agricultural visions and practices which lead to two concomitant philosophies of history and political practices. The former is rooted in the idea of "progress" and excludes *de jure* the essence of latter, which involves and presupposes the practice of *mercy*. This is why that man said: "Let both grow together until the harvest; at harvest time I will tell the reapers: 'Gather the weeds first and bind them in bundles to be burned, but gather the wheat into my barn'" (Matt 13:30). In fact, the Gnostic and Manichean views of a badly constructed world and the agnostic modern idea of an accumulative Progress are identically based in a quasi-Joachimite or Hegelian vision of the future as a *telos* that need not return to the *archê*, which can leave memory of the past behind in its self-justifying achievement of putative perfect spiritual justice. In the concrete world in which we live, sanctity and sin simultaneously grow

and are manifest. It is just this that excites God's patience—and what Saint Exupéry rejects.

The only inhabitant in B-612 does not wait. He faces up to obstacles. "The earth teaches us more about ourselves than all the books in the world, because it is resistant to us. Self-discovery comes when man measures himself against an obstacle," as the French pilot puts it.[10] Christian wisdom, by contrast, invites us to wait to the End: "If the farmer waits all winter, so much ought you to wait the final outcome of events, remembering who it is that ploughs the soil of our souls. […] And when I speak of the final outcome, I am not referring to the end of this present life, but to the future life and to God's plan for us, which aims to salvation and Glory."[11]

And what about stockbreeding on B-612? The little prince's desire for an animal cohabitant is in remarkable contrast with the Genesis narrative for which animals are created as part of the ecosystem of the Earth, each particularly named by Adam. The only real sign of integral relation in the prince's asteroid is the mysterious rose which once grew. The prince did indeed cultivate this rose, which he loved, but had to do so by making for her a glass container to separate her from the hostile environment of the asteroid. The relationship between the prince and the rose is the closest we come in the "genesis" of *Le Petit Prince*, to the nuptiality of Adam and Eve. But whereas Eve awoke the deepest humanity of Adam, revealing him

[9] *The Art of the Commonplace* (Berkeley: Counterpoint, 2003), 153.

[10] *Terre des hommes*, in *Oeuvres completes*, vol.1 (Paris: Gallimard, 1987), 171.
[11] Saint John Chrysostom, *On Providence*, 9.1.

to himself—"This one, at last, is bone of my bone and flesh of my flesh" (Gen 2:23)—the love-relation of the prince with the rose immediately falls into suspicion: the prince began to distrust that she was taking advantage of him, and so he resolved to divorce himself from his planet. And even when she apologized for her vanity and the two reconciled, she nevertheless encouraged him to go ahead with his journey of abandonment. All of this, we could say, is rooted finally in the fact of ultimate distinction between Le Petit Prince and the Christian vision: for the former, while there pretends to be children, there is not father. It is a narrative without paternity. While for the latter the whole sense of creation and meaning is based in the filial of bond. Just as this bond, arising from the common Father, makes all of the creatures of creation intimate with us, bringing about the "universal fraternity" referred to by Pope Francis (LS 228), attaining its particular configuration in the intimacy of man and woman, which does not cancel the sexual difference but enhances it (LS 155). Instead, even though the little prince acknowledges in the rose a longing for intimate communication, he experiences her as a different flesh and ends up by judging and repudiating her. The prince and the rose are not created beings: they have been thrown into time and this commonality in their being-there (*Dasein*), this common being-there-with-one-another (*Mitsein*), is not enough to lead them to communion, much less does it flow for an anterior Love that is the secret heart of being as the doctrine of the Trinity requires.

As much as the Genesis of the Bible and the "genesis" of Le Petit Prince are cases in contrast, at the same time they highlight the interrelation of world, love, nuptiality, and filial identity as the keystones of our sense of being. In this light it is worth noting that the genesis of love in the biblical narrative is one of fidelity, of the revelation of oneself to oneself, of correspondence and of communion. In Le Petit Prince, by contrast, love is modern: it is a game of suspicion, the freedom of which is only proved in the abandonment of the limitation of fidelity, and so in the negative freedom to abandon the other supposedly in the name of love. In the most profound sense, we see here the intimate interrelation between a personal view of creation, as opposed to the anonymous and abstract modern view of "environment." For the former, based in the constitutive filial relation of created being, love is the stuff of the intimate relation that sustains being, while for the latter things exist *before* relation, such that fatherhood is basically irrelevant and so is the interrelation of genuine communion of beings. There are plants and children in Le Petite Prince, but there is no paternity. The complex world of human genesis and interrelation with the Earth is wholly absent. Some years before writing his famous tale, the French pilot and writer had confessed: "Deprived of God too early, at the age when you still seek a refuge, we see ourselves as obliged to struggle for life as lonely little men."[12]

---

[12] *Carnets* (Paris: Gallimard, 1953), 35.

II

THE HEART OF THE CRITIQUE of the environmental crisis offered in *Laudato Si'* aims most directly at what Pope Francis calls "the dominant technocratic paradigm" (LS 101). What is this paradigm? It is the new heretofore-unthinkable anthropocentrism provoked by two centuries of technological advances by which humans have acquired an unprecedented power over themselves, a sense of self-sufficiency that has precisely eroded our vision of being as "filial," this is, as constitutively dependent, needy and limited. The modern human being, animated by the technological paradigm, is a fatherless human who aspires to perfect power over himself. Francis describes it like this:

> The technological paradigm . . . tends to absorb everything into its ironclad logic, and those who are surrounded with technology "know full well that it moves forward in the final analysis neither for profit nor for the well-being of the human race," that "in the most radical sense of the term power is its motive—a lordship over all."[13] (LS 108)

The "unrestrained delusions of grandeur" (LS 114) that the "technological paradigm" provokes leads to the ideological and spiritual delusion of being "fatherless," to the core satanic lie. This satanic lie, which reconfigures the self as "fatherless," is the true object of critique of *Laudato*

Si'. In a word: the ecological crisis, as Pope Francis analyzes it, is based on technological and ideological obfuscation of the paternal origin and filial nature of being. It is in fact the modern anthropocentrism of a purely secularized mode of being which "has paradoxically ended up prizing technical thought over reality, since 'the technological mind sees nature as an insensate order, as a cold body of facts, as a mere "given," as an object of utility, as raw material to be hammered into useful shape; it views the cosmos similarly as a mere "space" into which objects can be thrown with complete indifference'" (LS 115).[14] This self-sufficient anthropocentrism, which Francis analyzes as characteristic of modernity and the "technological paradigm," is also characteristic of the anthropological vision of *Le Petit Prince*.

As much as *Le Petit Prince* presents itself as a narrative of childhood, based on the leitmotif of the folly of "grown-ups" and the wisdom of "children," in actual fact there are no children or grown-ups in the tale, since there are no concrete relations between children and adults. One reads *Le Petit Prince* in vain for an evidence of filiation or paternity. *Le Petit Prince* is a paradigmatically fatherless story, and to that extent it is a childless story. The nameless characters here are not *related* to any concrete "grown-up"—a parent, an aunt, a teacher—neither, therefore, are they "children" in any concrete sense, since

13 Quoting Romano Guardini, *Das Ende der Neuzeit*, 63–64; ET: *The End of the Modern World*, 56.

14 Quoting Guardini, *Das Ende der Neuzeit*, 63.

they are not once identified as any-one's son, niece, pupil or otherwise. The basically abstract world of these self-sufficient "children" (modern anthropocentric beings) is in this way an eminently unrealistic world. The protagonist, crashed in the desert with the little prince, describes him like this: "My little man seemed neither to be straying uncertainly among the sands, nor to be fainting from fatigue or hunger or thirst or fear. Nothing about him gave any suggestion of a child lost in the middle of the desert, a thousand miles from any human hab-itation." Indeed he is not childlike at all; he is inhumanly self-sufficient. This self-sufficient ideal—characteris-tic of Saint Exupéry's "child"—is exactly the image of the modern anthropocentrism the Pope criticizes. And Saint Exupéry himself proposes it, as the mode of being necessary for secularized humanity. All of this leads us back to the question of ecology, and how *Laudato Si'* and *Le Petit Prince* offer two irreconcilable visions of the world and being.

To Saint Exupéry is frequently attributed the saying, "You do not inherit the earth from your ancestors: you borrow it from your children." Environmental groups often use this saying as a slogan. Whether it is origi-nal to Saint Exupéry or not, the saying is both iconic of his fatherless vision of humanity and representative of the ontology he presumes. The human being is, first of all, self-enclosed: a being for which the fragility of the child, who must first receive his being (and his name) from his father, is negated. This program is that of the project of being built for the future, rather than anteriorly received as a

child from the parents (cf. LS 159–162). It is perfectly captured in that most famous injunction of the fox: one must "make bonds" (*il faut créer des liens*). The little prince completes the injunction: we must "make bonds between men" (*entre les hommes*), between oneself and others, and in our context between our human selves and the created world. The ontological accent here lies wholly on the side of what the self-sufficing human being can *make*, what he can *do* for himself. He *hands on* the world, and so he must create the bonds of interrelation. Or, in another famous saying of Saint Exupéry: "True happi-ness comes from the joy of deeds well done." In all cases being is presumed to exist in a more or less self-enclosed and autonomous state, the activism of humans is what makes the world bet-ter or worse, happier or less, more interrelated or not. The integral ecol-ogy of Pope Francis is radically other-wise: humanity must, before the present crisis, shuffle off the "unre-strained delusions of grandeur," of self-sufficiency implied by the "tech-nological paradigm," and rediscover the always-prior givenness of being. The most elemental and first truth of being is being *from* the Father. And in this anterior givenness, where the filial nature of being as such is rediscov-ered, we find that we are truly sons in the Son, children interrelated with each other in the Word who spoke the whole of creation into being of the Father. From this epiphany surges a new vision of human being that is, finally, ecological in an integral sense.

III

POPE FRANCIS'S PROPOSAL for an "integral ecology" is founded on the sacramental depth of the world. This sacramental depth at once acknowledges and upholds the constitutive relation and difference of creation with regards the Creator, while it eschews every logic of separation that would construe these as dualistically related by a contrast and every logic of confusion that would interpret these as pantheistically or materialistically bound. To this end, *Laudato Si'* is at once radically anti-monist and anti-dualist, because its logical and ontological root is definitely Trinitarian. The antinomian oppositions undermined by post-modern "Deep Ecology," between created and uncreated, alive and inert, human and nonhuman, man and woman, will never be overtaken through a drastic separation, whether in a premodern (platonic or Gnostic) or modern (pseudo-Christian or agnostic) way, either through a pantheistic or agnostic unification. In this sense, *Laudato Si'* clearly affirms the paternal relation of reality as ontologically constituted in relation to an uncreated loving God (LS 76). Herein arises the key to the Pope's "integral ecology," in which the substantial communality of being, living and inert, human and non-human, male and female, arises directly from the recognition that God, because he is inter-relation of difference in unity, does not despise matter or creation (LS 98 and LS 235), but rather himself constitutes the fraternity of men and the communion of creation, the "universal fraternity" (LS 1 and LS 228).

The destructive "dominion" of modern anthropocentrism and the instrumentalist view of humanity with regard to the Earth will not be healed, either by the substituting of nature for creation (LS 76) or of biocentrism for anthropocentrism (LS 118). Neither will it be resolved by the refusal of the peculiar role and the novelty of human being among created beings (LS 81) or by the deification of the Earth (LS 90). These are the counterfeit ends (redemption) offered by Saint Exupéry's little prince and the gentle snake he finds by chance in the African desert.

On the Eighth Day, the snake and the little prince have a sad and nostalgic chat:

> "Good evening," said the little prince courteously.
>
> "Good evening," said the snake.
>
> "What planet is this on which I have come down?" asked the little prince.
>
> "This is the Earth; this is Africa," the snake answered.
>
> "Ah! Then there are no people on the Earth?"
>
> "This is the desert. There are no people in the desert. The Earth is large," said the snake.
>
> The little prince sat down on a stone, and raised his eyes toward the sky.
>
> "I wonder," he said, "whether the stars are set alight in heaven so that one day each one of us may find his own again... Look at my planet. It is right there above us. But how far away it is!"
>
> "It is beautiful," the snake said.
>
> "What has brought you here?"

"I have been having some trouble with a flower," said the little prince.

"Ah!" said the snake.

And they were both silent.

"Where are the men?" the little prince at last took up the conversation again. "It is a little lonely in the desert…"

"It is also lonely among men," the snake said.

The little prince gazed at him for a long time.

"You are a funny animal," he said at last. "You are no thicker than a finger…"

"But I am more powerful than the finger of a king," said the snake.

The little prince smiled.

"You are not very powerful. You haven't even any feet. You cannot even travel…"

"I can carry you farther than any ship could take you," said the snake. He twined himself around the little prince's ankle, like a golden bracelet.

"Whomever I touch, I send back to the earth from whence he came," the snake spoke again. "But you are innocent and true, and you come from a star…"

The little prince made no reply.

"You move me to pity—you are so weak on this Earth made of granite," the snake said. "I can help you, some day, if you grow too homesick for your own planet. I can."

"Oh! I understand you very well," said the little prince. "But why do you always speak in riddles?"

"I solve them all," said the snake. And they were both silent.[15]

After his hebdomadal odyssey (a nihilist de-creation), the prince real- izes that "it is lonely also among men" and that it is impossible to "create bonds between them," as the fox urged upon him in their first encounter.[16] The snake's redemptive offer is to send him back to the planet from which he came: a return to the eternal estate of orphanage. The little prince meekly offers his heel to be bitten by the serpent. Its venom will operate the "miracle."

For Adam and Eve, that other ancient snake had not the last word. What for a long time was taken as a curse was, in truth, the promise of redemption: "You [will] return to the ground, since from it you were taken; for dust you are and to dust you will return" (Gen 3:19). This return to the earth was never, we can now see, a death threat. To return to the original red mud amounts to a return to God's hands and to open the possibility of being reshaped again. And the way of this refashioning is the sacramental depth of creation, both transfigured by Christ's incarnation and already indigenous to the original act of creation. The Word took human flesh (originally made in his own image, after his own likeness), earthly biological flesh, built from chemicals of this Earth, two thousand years ago, in the last, the most unique and the most striking of theophanies. For God, to show himself is to empty himself of his divine form while remaining eternally who he *is* hypostatically. The divine *kênosis* (Phil 2:7) into the created world is an essential, and not an exceptional, characteristic of the God who invites the human being and the

---

[15] Antoine de Saint Exupéry, *The Little Prince*, Chapter xvii.

[16] Ibid., Chapter xxi.

entire creation through him to its definitive fulfillment: "Christ emptied himself, so that nature might receive as much of him as it could hold."[17] Christ empties himself of his divine form in order that the world might be caught up in his un-emptiable "I" before the Father. All that remains of "divinity" on the Cross is the eternal divine person of Son, and in this way the *kênosis* of the Son unwinds the falling way of creation, because it draws the falling of being into the darkness of the *nihil* now into the perfect dialog of the filiation from the Father. Christ thus occupies the center of the world: revealing in himself the original beauty of being, which is the irreducible communion of filiation, and thereby restoring creation's ultimate life. The definitive revelation and *kênosis* of the Son has taken place in the Earth. It has soaked the soil of created being with the outpouring of divine love. It has incarnated the Eternal into the human womb of a woman who is *of this Earth*. In doing so, the Incarnate Lord assures that the presence of the human animal among all the living of this Earth, has bestowed a unique destiny upon *this* planet, Earth, and upon *this* species, human. The human being, this Earth dweller, is the bearer of a singular and irreducible dignity, which in turn imbues his human home, the Earth, with singular and irreducible value (LS 43, LS 81, LS 83 and LS 90). We could say that, by this, the Earth has become a sacrament for the entire cosmos as the human species has been invested with a prophetic mission with regards all

personal life in the universe, if it ever were discovered beyond the bounds of our Earth.

Only a paradoxical sacramental view of the Earth can perform a real union without confusion or dissolution of oppositions: created-uncreated, alive-inert, human-nonhuman, and man-woman dismissing the slightest suspicion of Gnosticism or pantheism. As a sacrament, the Earth reveals the dimension of depth that is in all things, all created reality, that subsists in relation to the mysterious abyss of God himself. Creation as a sacrament is a *symbolon*, something that brings together and overtakes the abyss between two different and even opposed, although not divided, realities: that which sanctifies (the Creator-God) and that which is sanctified (the creation), the uncreated and the created, the transcendence and the immanence of God. Consequently, the paternal act of loving creation into being, maintaining it though the Fall and redeeming it by the Incarnation, makes of the soil of the Earth a true image of Heaven. The "integral ecology" Pope Francis proposes in *Laudato Si'* shows how the a real remembering of "origins" in the Christian tradition makes fresh connections and bridges that restore an ecological vision of creation capable of reconciling the apparent fissures that have provoked the neuroses of modernity and precipitated our current ecological crisis.

Finally, the high point where God is manifest in our planet, in the Earth, is the Eucharist. The Eucharist bridges the infinite difference between the divine Creator, on the one hand, and living and inert creation, on the other.

---

[17] Saint Gregory of Nyssa, *On the Psalms*, 3.

As such, it is the Eucharist, the bond, the *synaxis* that is anteriorly *given*, and not "made." The Eucharist is the received bond that binds human beings to each other and to the remainder of life and matter, as it binds us to the life of God himself. In the divine presence in bread and wine, on the Earth, two precise earthly and vegetal species, wheat and grape, give us simultaneously the truth of ourselves, the truth of creation and the truth of God. Wheat and grape, the work of an earthly yeast fungus which lives from transforming grapes' fructose into ethyl alcohol, the work of human hands grinding grain and making the flour, the fire wielded by the baker at the oven in which he bakes, all of this become the historical and material sacrament of the presence of God. Here is transcended the ontological abyss between created and uncreated; here the human being truly makes the bond he can only revive in the form of an anterior and gratuitous gift that does not depend upon him. What would happen if human beings ignored the Pope Francis's call to an "ecological conversion"? What would become of the human being if, on account of our negligence, wheat and grape disappear from the Earth? What would become of the Earth if, on account of our negligence, the human being were to become extinct? By the Incarnation of the Son of God, these are ecological diversities on which the existence and meaning of the entire universe is predicated.

He is Real, Jonathan McCormack, pen and ink

FRAGMENTS

Tyler DeLong

#1
On bended knee we waited.
Fr. Norbert, in a confusion set on by age (or maybe kindness), hands
    flipping through pages
Searching.
Searching-feeling for the words that transform matter (without which
    we cannot go on)
Silence growing.
All creation waiting on aged hands, to lift chalice up in words consecrating.
Eternity set still.
The snow falling on sill and glass, knowing all will go on.
It always does.
Thanks be to God.

#2
We watched overhead,
Sandhill cranes making their way to lake-beyond-trees.
In the fading light of evening,
Radiant under wing, we followed their flight—disappearing.

On autumn grass, chilled and beholden
We played—rolled—bison and wolves.
Becoming lost in play-learning, I lie under panting.
You were gored, hoof and horn (these hands become many).
Death came long-winded, you ate my flesh.
Resting upon my body, we lay

What curious embrace of children to father.
This must be before time.

#3
Two things which readily oppose one another,
Stand endlessly before my eyes, my mind
Broken by the chasm,
I want to hold them together.

Fleeing to the wild, witnessing
Wonder.
Nature overwhelmed with,
Substance becoming glory
Disposition
Transfigured to what it was before. Or,
At least closer.

Can I return to a city (children playing in alley not this forest)
To write of wilderness splendor—
It is terror indeed.
That feeling of infinite smallness.
Wrecking ideals and wounding to the heart.

Can my children play in those streets again?
Laying seed where concrete lies strangling.
But its hardness may be softened by children wild
Widening
Cracks.

Can the desert rejoice and blossom?
Can these be held together for a time?
Is it safe (not that we are now, for we are our own enemies, demons made
    real in isolation)?

TABOR

Devan Meade DeCicco

words are created things
        tabernacles

        not unnecessary
    it is not enough

letters could make a tent
grammar, a cherubim linen

the root cellar was lit
                by a single skylight
I checked the wine
        fermented
speaking in mysteries

between the dandelion
        the wild yeast
        and the honeycomb

        I could not see it
        I could not speak it

Do not tell anyone.

I stepped back out into afternoon sun
        squinted
        asked my wife
  who emerged from porch
where the children were
           she said they had made
    a fort of blankets and chairs
    and wanted a flashlight

I await the restoration
                of the phrase
so it may reveal itself
I await the restoration
                of the honey bee
        it groans

HYMNS TO THE NIGHT 5
(excerpt)

Novalis (1772–1801)

translated by
James R. Wetmore

Rolled away the stone,
All humankind arisen,
Ever thine, and thine alone
No longer fast in prison.
Autumnal cares are scattered
Thy golden grail before,
Earth and Life in one dish served
A last supper, then no more.

To wedding death does beckon,
The lamps all burning clear
The virgins in their places
Of want of oil, no fear.
O, that far-flung spaces
Rang thy coming nigh,
The stars to us a-calling
With human sound and sigh.

Unto thee, O Mary
Myriad hearts aspire
Lost among the shadows
You their sole desire.
From thee they hope for healing
'Mid their anxious hearts' unrest
Wouldst thou, O Holy Creature
But clasp them to thy breast.

Inner fires burning,
Troubles keen upon our chest,
Away from this world yearning
In thy harbor seek we rest.
Thy help to us fair flowing
Quells poverty and pain,
Draws forth our soul-deep seeking
With thee always to remain.

At gravesides weep in torment
None with loving faith full-brim'd,
For Love, such sweet possession!
From their hearts can n'er be trimmed.
O! to salve our unmet longings,
Now nears the mystic Night
Peopled full with spirits true
To trim our wicks new-bright.

Be strong, for we are striving,
To endless life we're bound,
Our inner souls' glow spreading,
Into spirit-senses crowned.
Then out the starry vineyard press'd
Streams golden living wine
And we who raise a cup and drink
As new-lit stars shall shine.

Love's then freely given,
Separation is no more,
All of life a single surge,
A sea without a shore.
One Night—one Night all rapture,
One everlasting Poem,
One Sun, our Sun, the Sun of all,
The Face of God, our Home.

SOLESMES BELLS

Philippa Martyr

The deeps came alive in your tongues
The depth-sounding whale song
Counterpoint bursting iron bubbles
The great bell rang, advancing
Like Saturn, cold and old and relentless
Turning solemnly in space, back and round
And bearing-down and never-ending
Other voices joined you
But at the end your voice alone remained
I came alive to the Christ-like thrill of your song
Surfacing from the green deeps
They rang inside me for hours afterwards

The Benthic & the Celestial

Scott F. Martin

"*I believe in God the Father Almighty, maker of heaven and earth, of all things visible and invisible.*"
～ The Nicene Creed

"*We're seeing wonders while they're seeing dust.*"
～ Ballydowse "The Didge Song"

N UNSEEN WORLD exists all around us. Actually, two unseen worlds. One is invisible and the other is generally unseen. Both are accessible, though effort is required to see either.

Near you in a pond or a river, beneath the blanket of water, attached to the underside of rocks, buried in the silt, in the pockets of fallen logs, they wait, feed, grow, and change.

Benthic macroinvertebrates inhabit the unseen world. They are bugs in the river-bed to put it baldly. It is another and different world, a world where insects spend their "childhood" and crustaceans, mollusks, annelids, and other taxa spend most or all of their lives. Not to mention the vertebrate denizens as well.

What's fascinating is that all this abundant life—if water quality is not compromised—exists below the liquid surface, beneath our ignorance.

Dragonfly nymphs lying in wait for prey to grasp and devour. Caddisfly larvae with their endless variety of cases made from sand and pebbles, decayed wood, and shredded leaves where they live until metamorphosis and become creatures of the air. Scuds swimming sideways, bloodworms squirming, water scorpions walking on long, spindly legs, hellgrammites clinging to the cobble, and water pennies crawling on submerged logs: all these inhabit rivers and ponds, and the list, while not endless, goes on like a Biblical genealogy.

In Eastern Christianity, January 6th is Theophany; the time when Western-rite Christians celebrate Epiphany. This commemorates Jesus's baptism which in turn blessed all the waters of the world.

When aquatic biodiversity is present, the waters are doubly blessed by God's providence.

How often have we stood knee-deep in water ignorant of the myriad life just below our toes? How unaware are we of the invisible activity in Heaven (and in the material realm) of God, angels, saints, and of loved ones who served Jesus on earth? How much of the Kingdom of Heaven is working by our side while we go about our mundane tasks and pleasures?

I attended a "summer camp" for teachers a few years back and worked with the Michigan Department of Natural Resources to see what wildlife conservation is all about (granted, the DNR focuses on game wildlife, but helping one species quite often benefits others).

The Thursday of that week we spent the day with the fisheries division. The afternoon found us hiking along the white cedar-lined banks of the Au Sable, the "Holy Waters" of northern lower Michigan. We joined a skiff in the water that held an AC generator and some other equipment. We cautiously strolled through the tannin-stained water until we found the suitable habitat. We plunged long rods beneath the water's surface, connected to the generator, to activate the magic. The ends of the rods had an anode. Pressing a button on the rod sent AC electrical current through the anode into the flowing water all around us, though our waders kept us immune to its effects.

Looking around, one might have concluded that the river was devoid of animal life as none could be spotted. But with the button depressed, stunned creatures appeared out of nowhere, floating to the surface. Brook and brown trout with white bellies up, crayfish, and other aquatic fauna, anything sizable all rose as if summoned and astounded by their creator. While stunned they could be easily scooped up, measured, and if necessary tagged as a measure of population, health, or whatever metric once could desire to assess the river. Sure, we were stream shocking, as it's called, for fish, but without an abundance of macroinvertebrates there would be no fish.

It's no exaggeration to have felt awe at the power of technology properly harnessed, at the wonder of creatures, and for those with the imaginations to grasp, the blanket of grace.

The English translation of the Nicene Creed was revised not long ago. The end of the first section about God the Father had read that he was the "maker of heaven and earth of all things *seen and unseen*." The last phrase "seen and unseen" was changed to "visible and invisible" to clarify the difference between the natural and supernatural realms.

Attending a winter meditation at a Jesuit retreat center on the banks of the Rouge River, I happened to spot a muskrat gathering grasses while the rest of the group was focusing on the words of St. John of the Cross. Whereas the angels who may have been guarding us against demonic attack remained invisible no matter where my attention may have been drawn.

Grace is present in both cases.

If we can learn to see, appreciate, and love the benthic macroinvertebrates unseen in our watersheds, we might increase our faith in the invisible in Heaven.

Perhaps the riffles on the surface and the cobble and decomposing leaf litter beneath are thin places not restricted to a particular locale? Perhaps they are icons not made with hands?

Loving our neighbors should not be a globalized abstraction. We are meant to love our literal neighbors and some of those neighbors may not be human. They may not even be the charismatic megafauna that most children love. They may possess pincers, mandibles, and exoskeletons. We are called to love the leper and the midge, after all the Lord we love made them both.

"There lives the dearest freshness deep/ down things" even the ugly, the frightening, and the creepy-crawly. Though they live some or all of their life in the unseen world, they were placed here by the invisible world. Its reasons may not always be clear, but they have their place and we are charged with keeping them.

Monks Break the Earth, Matthew Livermore,
linocut

THREE POEMS

Tom Sturch

BLUE HOUR

Before night's dumb language
        lies exposed
And its dreams of day cease
        their grappling in the throat,
Sleep dies, disturbed
        by stirring birds, by gentler
Thoughts more worthy.

        So from this stilted repose
I rise and dress to contemplate
        in the stand of a nearby slough
The early praise of tree frogs
        and cardinals.
Climb, climb, the amphibians say,
        as dawn's honey-drenched rite
Flows down the cypress-pillared
        cathedral wood.

And the red birds in high branches
        raise their fernbrake
Antiphonals.

ON ROCKS AND CLOUDS

I believe the mountains rise to watch the long horizons,
beholding a steady state of ecstatic perfection, in bright conversation
for what is moving, elusive and gone;

this, since I was six and climbed the rock dam at the mill pond to watch
the snapping turtles, their stoic voids in the rippling sun, that
would slip beneath the glimmer at a pebble's splash;
this, an instruction that to venture upon their pleasure was a ritual kept
in reverent procession, step by conscious step—fixed to gain
from merest glimpse, desire for lasting communion;
this, now at sixty, to teach clouding eyes to hold lightly what they see
and from familiar footing on those long converging memories,
treasure the heightened anticipation of vanishing.

WOODSMAN

My grandfather bore the arms
of a carpenter and the back
of a tenement farmer
and I sat upon his shoulders.
He'd lumber through the forest,
his walking stick a pendulum
taking measures of the earth.
His hair was spice and leather.
Our quest: the hidden panther,
and he grunted as we climbed.
He'd point to scat and paw print.
He'd catch flashes of its withers
and sight his goad on the deep
between a rock and a leaning pine.
And under a gathering granite sky
we heard the forest groaning.
He said it was the strength
of the wood on the wind. Listen,
how it gives and bends and
within, it hides the panther.
And he'd smell the air and
tell the time till rain.
I am aloft and bending.
I hear the far off thunder.
I clasp my hands beneath his chin.
I become our eyes and ears,
holding to the words he says.
And all the world is wonder.

TALKING WITH YOUR HANDS / DUENDE DANCE

Isak Bond

> In another life
> you would have danced
> flamenco, held the gleaming knife
> to every mortal throat that chanced
> the down dark deep,
> the panic and the fitful sleep
> of every man entranced
> by black dreams and holy visions, rife
> with what you keep
> a secret in the strife
> of striking heels glanced
> upon the floor beneath your skirt sweep.
>
>> A fiery glow upon your face,
>> you stare into a separate place.
>
> As deliberate and bold
> as birds of prey, your hands
> would have woven patterns old
> as tales of floods and fertile lands,
> of flaming swords
> and gleaming hoards
> of gold and jewels, buried in the sands
> of islands in the oceans, cold
> and limitless, the unexplored
> and dark untold
> arenas under dread commands
> more terrible than what your dance affords.
>
>> Amen, amen I say to you,
>> ask the dusk what you should do.
>
> Here and now, your eyes of mirth
> and breath as quick as rain
> on roof hint your words are sounds of earth,

but your hands are the domain
of heaven's movements; high
and low together cry
the wild mischief match; the plain
muddy spoken word worth
very little, and the spry
unruly gesture giving birth
the possibility of death, a stain
to baptize all you say a very pretty lie.

Word Hunger

Elias Crim

"The Formalist school represents an abortive idealism applied to the question of art. The Formalists show a fast ripening religiousness. They are followers of St. John. They believe that 'In the beginning was the Word.'"

LEON TROTSKY, "Literature and Revolution" (1924)

1. Cultural resistance

As IN THE TIMES OF Russian poet Mandelstam (1891–1938), we find ourselves today amidst *friends and enemies of the word.*

A genuine poet merely trying to live inside Stalin's dark gulag empire in the 1930s, Mandelstam (through the memoirs of his remarkable wife Nadezhda) commented mordantly on the condition of the official culture of the USSR:

> With one exception . . . all my informants [i.e., government informers] have at least been well intentioned. The exception was a certain Tiufiakov, who used to come and see me in Ulianovsk at the beginning of the fifties, before Stalin's death. Tiufiakov behaved monstrously toward me. He was a member of the literature faculty at the Teachers' Training College and deputy director of it. A war veteran, he was covered with medals for his service as a political officer, and he loved to read war novels which described the execution of cowards or deserters in front of their units. He had devoted the whole of his life to the "reconstruction of higher education," and for this reason he had not had time to take any degrees himself. He was a typical Komsomol of the twenties who had then made a career as a "permanent official."

> He had been relieved of teaching duties so that he could devote all his time to watching over "ideological purity," the slightest deviation from which he duly reported to the right quarters. He was transferred from college to college, mainly to keep an eye on directors suspected of "liberalism."

> Apart from Tiufiakov, there was also Glukov, whose name should be recorded for posterity. This man had received a medal for his part in the deportation of the kulaks, and had also been awarded a doctorate for a dissertation on Spinoza. He performed his duties in quite open fashion, summoning students to his office and instructing them whom they should get up and denounce at meetings, and in what terms.

Culture worship can easily become transmogrified into a mask for repression, as we learn from these memoirs describing a time when people could be killed for poetry—"a sign of unparalleled respect," as Nadezhda Mandelstam writes, "because they are still capable of living by it."

The true sense of culture, of cultural growth as it has been known for generations, she observes, is connected with the harvesting of the fields and the "spores of culture" which keep civilization alive. The ancients saw the seed as a principle of existence: they felt a natural awe at the processes of generation and extinction, and before blood and water.

For the lover of words, the philologue in the deepest sense, culture is also a matter of roots, as Mandelstam would have argued. ("Our Acropolis," he once claimed, "is Vladimir Dahl's dictionary," referring to the great etymological work, the Russian-language OED.)

In M.'s [her husband's] eyes "philology" was a profound concept of moral importance—the word, after all, is Logos, the embodiment of all meaning. A people—and this applies to the Russian people—exists only while it possesses the living word, the word untouched by necrosis…the realm of dead words shorn of meaning, good only as a means of doping the people. A living word—in the church, the family, or in the company of the friends and fellow poets who formed his circle and upheld the same values—this was what M. hoped to find in Petersburg in 1920.

It is this unapologetic sense of the logos which separates the "friends of the word" from the technical philologists. Thus Trotsky's attack (in his essay "Literature and Revolution") on the former for their lack of a properly materialistic-positivistic aesthetic.

✠✠✠

We should of course be wary of overwrought historical comparisons. The situation of word lovers in America today is quite different in many respects from that of writers and intellectuals in 1930s Stalinist Russia.

As Neil Postman argued thirty years ago, the danger we face turns out not to be Orwellian, that is, a world of book burning and externally imposed repression, perhaps leading to the gulag. It is instead Huxleyan, a *soma*-imbibing dreamscape in which there is no reason to ban a book because no one wants to read one. Instead of Orwell's censorship, Huxley saw us drowning in information leading to passivity and mere egoism. Not a captive culture so much as a trivial culture, built upon our almost infinite appetite for distraction.

And just as Postman described, we Americans have made an historical progression through paradigmatic cities—from Boston (during the Revolution) through New York (during 19th century immigration), Chicago (industrialization) leading to today's Las Vegas (the shrine of spectacle)—now consummated in the election of casino-builder Trump.

And thus it is we find Mandelstam's memoirs speaking to us. We have cheerfully constructed our own mental gulag, an elaborate digital prison—let us call it "The Platform"—which induces a kind of attention deficit disorder fatal to any sustained contemplation and (Josef Pieper would argue) to genuine culture. The Platform is proving to be a critical tool of mass control, a logical extension of advertising and consumerist ideology.

Soviet-era readers of *Pravda* and other official publications liked to say they learned to read their news "upside-down"—i.e., by assuming that whatever the regime claimed had happened was in fact the opposite of the facts. The documentaries of British filmmaker Adam Curtis—*Century of the Self* and now *Hypernormalisation*—trace the way in which this new gulag—the first such penal institution ever populated entirely by volunteers!—was put into place, one in which our *nomenklatura* exercise growing ability to create whatever fact-free reality may be called for.

As both McLuhan and Postman have taught us, a technology is never merely neutral: each brings its own innate consequences. The Platform is thus designed to create image, fantasy, therapy and, as Czeslaw Milosz observed, "a refusal to remember."

2. Deep reading

"Ecce dies veniunt, dicit Dominus Deus, et mittam famem in terram, non famem panis neque sitim acquae, sed audiendi verbum Domini."
(Amos 8:11, Vulgate edition)

[Behold, the days come, saith the Lord God, that I will send a famine in the land, not a famine of bread, nor a thirst for water, but of hearing the words of the Lord.
(KJV)]

LOVERS OF THE WORD as were Mandelstam and his friends, face a kind of internal emigration which requires not necessarily physical withdrawal from society but certainly an effort to disenthrall ourselves from our atopia, our shared fake place. Many of us have recognized this much at least.

The next step toward wholeness is a reach across time, in order to hear other voices. Mandelstam, still within a heavily oral culture, is again a guide here. His special word for "reader" in Russian is always *sobesednik*, literally, a collocutor, a person one converses or communes with. In his great essay on Dante, Mandelstam exhibits his gift (one shared with fellow poet Anna Akhmatova) of bridging time and space when reading the work of dead poets, noting the way the Italian poet greets his ancient models from antiquity in the Inferno. (We might recall here that the medievals spoke of *voces paginarum*, voices in the pages, hearing the authors.)

Now it is perhaps Mandelstam himself whose writings have an urgency—like that of Dante's Count Ugolino seizing his last chance to be heard among the living!—for us, if we are to avoid seeing the Logos vanish entirely from a world in which there is no longer any room for it.

I suggest that these voices can best be recovered by a form of deep reading, a fervent *ignis lectionis*: call it the mood of Milton's *Il Penseroso*.

The skills of deep reading, all of them originating in the study of sacred texts, include:

• *Grammar*: We should recall that the earliest missionaries were often grammarians. The ninth-century Abbot Smaragdus saw *grammatica speculativa* as a path to heaven, partly through its effect as a curb to our pride. We acquire the humility of learning the *rudimenta*, the *aleph beis*. Then there's also the curious cognate connections of the Latin word *grammatica* with grimoire and glamour—a further suggestion of mystical forces at work in the words.

• *Memorization*: From the rabbinical schools, note the Hebrew term *haga*, to pronounce aloud and so learn by heart.

• *Contemplation*: The medievals called this *ruminatio*, a thoughtful chewing-over of the text in order to gradually incorporate the words. Mystical commentators from both traditions have cited Psalm 34:8 in speaking of the heavenly bread: "O taste and see that the Lord is good…" The Talmudic commentators said of a scholar completely inward with his text, "He has eaten the book."

Our capacity for deep reading depends not only upon certain skills but also favorable conditions such as having a place set aside for such activity: a house of study, a *beit midrash*.

Once we are seated before the text, a moment of recollection is needed. We might recall the words, *Fuge, tace, quiesce* ("flee, be silent, quiet yourself"), an ancient apothegm of Christian spirituality. The ideal of *hesychia*, or integral silence, was characteristic of Egyptian and Palestinian eremitism in the early centuries AD. "The strength of monks," asserted the 12th-century religious Adam Scot, "is their silence" (*vigor claustralium quies eorum*), referring to a tradition already six centuries old.

In summary, let us take the relevant advice of Solomon ibn Gabirol, the 11th-century Andalusian poet and Jewish philosopher with a Neoplatonic bent: "In seeking wisdom, the first stage is silence, the second listening, the third remembrance, the fourth practicing, and fifth teaching."

The latter stages should become part of the methodology of the new institutes of cultural survival—perhaps MacIntyrean in inspiration—within which the point is not to separate ourselves from the unclean but rather uniquely to cultivate the spores of culture, the *logos spermatikos*.

3. Heavenly labials in a world of gutterals

I F THE DEEPEST reading resides in sacred texts, then we must hear those words in the original languages.

And at least in the case of Vulgate Latin (the language of Western Scripture from Jerome to well into the 20th century), the relative simplicity of the language makes its beauty quickly apparent, even to the reader with very little Latin, as in the great penitential Psalm 130, with its groundbass of *Domine, Domine* and *anima mea*:

> *De profundis clamavi ad te, Domine;*
> *Domine, exaudi vocem meam. Fiant*
>   *aures tuæ intendentes*
> *in vocem deprecationis meæ.*
> *Si iniquitates observaveris, Domine,*
>   *Domine, quis sustinebit?*
> *Quia apud te propitiatio est; et*
>   *propter legem tuam sustinui te,*
>   *Domine.*
> *Sustinuit anima mea in verbo ejus:*
> *Speravit anima mea in Domino.*

[Out of the depths have I cried unto thee, O Lord.
Lord, hear my voice: let thine ears be attentive to the voice of my supplications.
If thou, Lord, shouldest mark iniquities, O Lord, who shall stand?
But there is forgiveness with thee, that thou mayest be feared.
I wait for the Lord, my soul doth wait, and in his word do I hope.
                    (KJV)]

One friend of the word whose very conversion owed much to her reading of such texts was Simone Weil. Her fierce love of ancient Greek finally brought her to the Our Father in that language, after which she made it her life prayer, becoming for her a vehicle of a regular mystical experience:

> I had made a practice of saying it through once each morning with absolute attention. . . . Although I experience it each day, it exceeds my expectation at each repetition. . . .
>   At times the very first words tear my thoughts from my body and transport it to a place outside space where there is neither perspective nor point of view. The infinity of the ordinary expanses of perception is replaced by an infinity to the second or sometimes the third degree. At the same time, filling every part of this infinity of infinity, there is silence, a silence which is not an absence of sound but which is the object of a positive sensation, more positive than that of sound. Noises, if there are any, only reach me after crossing the silence.

How to account for this experience, given our cramped, busy modern imaginations? Sacred language surely has an incarnational dimension which insists we at certain times avoid ersatz bread (translations) in order to dine on *panis angelicus*, even in the company of what the tradition sometimes thought of as angel-mentors (as with Rabbi Joseph Karo's *maggid* with whom he studied Torah).

Historically this deep reading is mostly a matter of the main biblical languages: Hebrew, koine Greek, and Latin. Other languages of scripture— Aramaic, Syriac, Armenian, Georgian, Coptic, Ethiopic, and Paleo-Slavic—

are unknown to me but doubtless contain sound-worlds and spiritual landscapes of great beauty.

It is primarily in encountering (that is, hearing!) the religious texts of our tradition that we learn (partly out of necessity, given the linguistic challenges) what slow reading means and how we might become adept at it.

I cannot claim to have experienced the kind of mystical effects that came over Weil after she entered into the sacred linguistic space of the Our Father (or that of George Herbert's poem "Love," during one recitation of which she claimed to have a direct experience of Christ). I do take heart from her "Intimations of Christianity among the Ancient Greeks" when I remember a college afternoon many years ago talking with an older friend, a classics major.

I asked him what led him to study Greek. By way of reply, he suddenly began chanting Sappho's "Hymn to Aphrodite": "*Poikilothron athanat' Aphrodita…*" Spellbound like one of Odysseus' crew hearing the sirens' song, I signed up for Greek myself soon thereafter.

I should add that the movement from the intimations in Sappho's hymn to my first recitation of the Hail Mary (in Latin and English) took quite a number of years. But something led me there. For lovers of the word, the music is always there, always waiting to be heard.

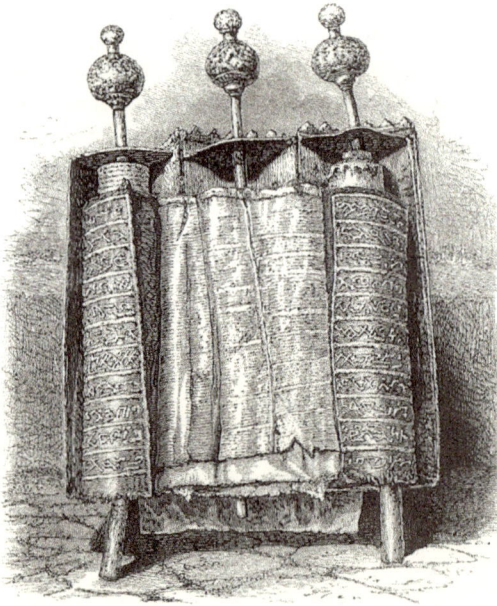

TWO POEMS

Francis Valentine

THE WOOD, THE WATER, THE WINE

the frogs started to sing in the cold of Lent
anticipating wonder and defiant of snow
dry oak leaves rattled from their branches
resilient in their stubborn deaths
and I pruned the wayward tangle of the grapevines
scraped their hairy trunks with a Buck knife
to expose the somnolent worms to sunlight
and the ravenous starlings

sparkling...
the wind across the pond
codes of prophecy   angelic ciphers
written in shining and light
the man of the water makes mouths at me
pebbles the color of seaweed are his eyes
clouds   dead flowers   somnolescence

we bottled four gallons of blackberry wine in August
for our pleasure and observance at Easter
but the money ran out in January
and we drank the lot before the Fast
the pear wine, comfortless and thin, still waited in bottles
weighted thick with lees and dead yeast
sallow and indifferent to hope
this is my transfiguration, this my alchemical tribute
look to my eyes, o spirits of Waterloo Township
look to my eyes, my mouth, the color of my blood

THE FISHER KING

"Moonstruck," they said.
"Angel-humped" is more like it.
I can do nothing but sit
in this boat all day
with my rod in my hands.
Don't smirk.
Self-pleasure is not an option:
an erection would be a welcome
rising from the dead.
Anyway, so I sit here,
rod in hand
(I'm too weak to cast)
dragging some worms behind the boat
while my butler, Sebastian, paddles.
It's called trolling,
but we never catch any trolls (haha)
just a trout every now and again.
We drink bad wine from a bladder
until the sun sends spikes
though my brain.
Then we go home where he reads
to me from *The Book of Prophecies*,
a melodrama of homunculi,
centaurs, and hermaphrodites—
the usual monsters and disasters.
Too boring for words.
Sometimes at night I dream
about the metal angel.
He comes with his sword
of bronze glowing red
and sears the pupils
from my eyes.
Sure it hurts,
but it gives me a hard-on,
at least in the dream.
I wake to the usual pains,
the uncertainties,
the predictable despair.
If I hadn't heard the voice
of God once, I'd swear
he didn't exist.

On the Edge of the Unthinkable

James R. Wetmore

AN INTERVIEW WITH OWEN BARFIELD

HIS PREVIOUSLY UNPUBLISHED INTERVIEW was originally conceived as a conversation with someone for whom I had the highest regard, and who seemed providentially qualified to advise me at that moment in my life. The year was 1996, and, at 44 years old, I was orienteering through the shadows of a variously dappled dark wood. For many years I had been an avid student of Rudolf Steiner. My entry into Steiner's work had been through his early epistemological studies, particularly those on what has come to be called Goethean science. Owen Barfield, I discovered, had followed a similar trajectory—nearly three quarters of a century earlier! I had read all his works, most closely those directly concerned with these themes: *Saving the Appearances: A Study in Idolatry*; *Romanticism Comes of Age*; *What Coleridge Thought*; and *The Rediscovery of Meaning*. I had discovered that Barfield had done for the little-known scientific work of Samuel Taylor Coleridge what Steiner had done for the better-known scientific work of Johann Wolfgang von Goethe. Both these faithful thinkers had practiced "spiritual science," and in so doing, quantified Quality and qualified Quantity. Knit together with these themes was the one that, in the end—as Barfield himself never tired of repeating—was really his *only* theme: the evolution of consciousness. Our conversation graciously became a spiritual counseling session.

Years later, there came to my attention, simultaneously, the work *Meditations on the Tarot: A Journey into Christian Hermeticism* (by an anonymous author now known to have been Valentin Tomberg) and several works by René Guénon, the *chef d'école* of a remarkable group of authors often referred to as the Traditionalists or Perennialists. That Guénon's magnum opus was entitled *The Reign of Quantity* sounded an echo in me, though I knew well enough there could be no more contrasting stances than that of Barfield, representing the standpoint of an evolution of consciousness, and that of Guénon, for whom such an idea was anathema. Tomberg seemed to occupy a middle ground.

The fruitful tension between these four authors expressed itself in my personal life. I became involved in the translation and editing of Rudolf Steiner's works, taught in a Waldorf school (based on the pedagogy he founded), and raised two Waldorf teachers. I established the imprint Polarity Press to republish many of Barfield's works. I founded the imprint LogoSophia to publish several of Tomberg's works. I became so immersed in Perennialism that I undertook, and in the end completed, the publication, under the imprint Sophia Perennis, of the

23-volume *Collected Works of René Guénon*, along with works of many related authors.

Then, in the 1990s, I discovered that in several of his works Barfield had cited Guénon appreciatively, notwithstanding the gap yawning between their points of view. By this time the question of "tradition" (vertical, static, eternal, ontological, simultaneous, absolute, *atma, purusha*…) as contrasted with "evolution" (horizontal, dynamic, temporal, cosmological, sequential, infinite, *maya, prakriti*…), was no head-spun diversion of the mind-intellect, but a deeply-felt conundrum of the eye of the heart. I did not even know whether Barfield was still living—most probably not, as his birth year was 1898! I had first met him in the 1970s, and knew he lived at the Walhatch, a home for the elderly in East Sussex, close by Emerson College, the primary center for training Waldorf teachers in the UK. A few calls yielded Barfield's phone number, and I rang him up. Barfield was ninety-eight-years old. He picked up the phone on the second ring. We talked. He invited me to come speak about "all the above," if I could get to him "while he was still good for an hour's conversation." Here was someone I revered (C.S. Lewis famously said of Barfield that a hundred years hence he would be the one remembered as a truly seminal thinker, not Lewis himself). I hastily assembled and posted a parcel of books, called a travel agent (that's what one did back then), and was soon through the doors of the Walhatch.

It was not a formal interview, but, at least for me, a heart-to-heart encounter. We dove right in, and spoke for that hour he was good for. Barfield was dressed in tweed, sipped a cup of tea, and offered me his full attention. Afternoon light slanted in, at once crisp and warm—and seeming poised to splay into little spectrums at the edges of the aged, mullioned windows. Several times he jumped up (in an age-appropriate fashion) to pull a volume from his wall of books. There were some pensive minutes during which he confided how difficult it was to have attained so great an age, mentioning that Lewis, perhaps his dearest friend, had died over 30 years before. He said also that the most unsettling thing for him at present was that, although he had difficulty remembering many things—especially recent events—he often felt assailed by unbidden childhood memories.

And so it went, with such asides leavening the primary theme. He said he was sorry he could not help me as much as I might have hoped, that he had many of the same questions—and how wonderful it would have been had we struck up a correspondence decades earlier (at which I kicked myself within, for I had considered just this, but hadn't wanted to presume). At a certain stage, where we felt awed at a sounding brink, Barfield—a man of exceeding literary and spiritual stature but hampered in speech with an ever-invasive stammer—grew animated and fairly blurted out: "This deserves a pipe!" and soon his freshly-tamped bowl was aglow. Then he leaned forward and said with—if there can be such a thing—a grave twinkle, "We're on the edge of the unthinkable here, you and I." Whence the title of my offering to this flagship issue of *Jesus the Imagination*.

It only remains to say that after that conversation I returned to my room and reconstructed every word I could, working far into the night. Along the way the notion pressed in upon me that, personal as it was, what had passed between the two of us might well speak to others too. Next morning I rang Barfield up and asked if I might drop off my notes for him to review and authenticate, as I had the sense they might help gird others tilting on similar fields. This he generously did, and the result was consigned to a drawer—but for the occasional fortifying re-read—until now. It seems a good sign that this "interview" from twenty-one years ago appears in print now quite literally as it comes of age. May it speak to you as it has to me. ~ JRW

JRW: It seems to some that there are two Barfields, one a literary critic and Coleridge scholar, intimate of C.S. Lewis and the Inklings, who, no matter where he casts his net (poetry, philology, history of science, epistemology, imagination, Scholastic metaphysics, etc.) always comes up with the same haul: evidence for an evolution of consciousness. And more than this: a metaphysic for this evolution—contradictory though this sounds—that involves a polarity in the changing significance of the subject-object distinction. This you are always careful to couch in "respectable" terms, though you permit yourself occasional reference to the "other" Barfield, even in the academic milieu: the Barfield who for more than seventy years has been a close student of Rudolf Steiner. This second Barfield claims that individual human consciousness, if it can begin to make its own the full depth of the imaginative faculty that underlies its experience of itself and the world, is the stage on which the drama of redemption will occur; he claims, in fact, that in overcoming the polarity of self and world through accomplishing a "turning-inside-out" of this polarity, we become conscious agents in the great return, the "spiritualization of matter" that is finally the same as the "union without confusion" of the return to God. Too much said too generally! Can you help sort this out?

OB: Actually, it would be more true to say that I began by being profoundly changed while reading poetry, and it would be more accurate to say that the essence of my work—apart from all the later associations—represents a deduction from what can happen when one reads poetry. I hope this doesn't sound too mundane. That I became an exponent of the evolution of consciousness was due to my experience of literature, especially poetry. And it happened that I was exposed to Rudolf Steiner's work at a very opportune moment in my own development. I quickly saw that my intimations on the subject were as nothing compared to Steiner's vast work.

JRW: Let's back up a moment. Much is said these days about "tradition," the loss of metaphysical principles, the deviation of individualism, the dis-enchanting of nature, and so forth. On the other hand, there are many movements (most spurious, some serious) trying to recall "tradition" in some form or another. Most popular just now seem to be non-Christian (or pre-Christian, especially "pagan") forms, though the appeal of ancient (hence, purportedly, truer) forms of Christianity, especially Orthodoxy, seems to be growing. Since the term "evolution" has proven central to your work, we might describe the fundamental difference in perspective at work here as that between *evolutionists* and *devolutionists*. The latter tend to see the course of history, especially Western history since the medieval age, as a deviation from traditional principles, and to discern no final good in the morass of unprincipled individualism, with its relativizing of all things, that has come to hold sway. I see on your bookshelf titles by René Guénon, and so you no doubt know that this view has been powerfully stated in our century by the so-called "traditionalists," including such other thinkers as Frithjof Schuon, Titus Burckhardt, Huston Smith, S.H. Nasr, etc. The evolutionists (and for you Steiner would be the prime example here, I presume) see

the loss of tradition and the rise of individualism, with a concurrent alienation of the self and despiritualizing of nature, as a necessary *precondition* for the development of moral freedom, without which love, and man's return to God *intact*, so to speak, would not be possible. That is, "to light one's own lamp" requires the impetus of experienced darkness, and the real possibility of perdition— something not conceivable, some would say, in a view where God simply returns to Himself through a haze of illusion He Himself creates, with no clear final end in view.

OB: Well, the devolutionary, or Guénonian position, boiled down to its essence, implies an endless recurrence of cycles, and the individual doesn't seem to have any positive significance.

JRW: The Traditionalist or Perennialist position would claim that the cycles begin with a Golden Age, and that the great Traditions only arose when our consciousness was sufficiently distanced from spiritual reality that we needed to be "reminded" from without. With our increasing forgetfulness, more and more concrete religious forms became necessary, and eventually, in our willful disregard, all traditional attachments were dissolved. We then entered upon the chaos of the modern age. When this process has reached its term there must be some final dissolution before the onset of a new Golden Age.

OB: I just don't see what the question is. What is this earlier spiritual consciousness? If there is no positive result during the cycle, then the ideal must be represented by its beginning, by some kind of collective, undifferentiated consciousness. You have to be clear about your terms. Do you mean that "individuals," in our current sense, were around in the Golden Age, somehow united with spiritual reality but still individual? If not, then the movement toward individuality during the cycle cannot simply be written off as a "devolution." Spiritual awareness is no virtue if there is no virtuous individual who is its subject. Spiritual in some sense this consciousness may have been, but it was not *self-conscious*. If individuality breaks with tradition and represents a final falling away toward "nothingness" as some kind of limit, then I suppose the ideal must seem to be a reversion to the earlier state of non-individualized consciousness. But can one seriously hold to such a position?

JRW: It is difficult to express these things. The Perennialist view has an extraordinary depth and clarity, but you're saying that it leaves out the significance of the movement toward individuality? Or sees it at any rate as a deviation only?

OB: It comes down to the function of freedom in the generality of things. Freedom is meaningless without a free agent. If the Perennialists wish to be consistent, then freedom is an illusion. The ideal would then seem to be some pre-individualized state! Or, you might say that only God is free, individuals being illusory in the final analysis. I realize what a host of subtleties and precisions one can become entangled in here. The evolutionary view

on the other hand (and I've tried to make this clear in one way or another in all of my books), which also envisages a non-individualized initial state, sees the movement toward individuation as the very *meaning* of the cosmic process.

JRW: In your *Saving the Appearances: A Study in Idolatry* you discuss this subject in some detail. What makes your argument so difficult is that it is not only a question of individuality arising (or "falling") from a non-individualized state, for you speak there more from the point of view of such polarities or complementarities as subject-object or self-world. We find it very difficult not to see everything in some such terms of inner-outer, all of which *already presume* some trace of individualizing subjectivity.

OB: It's only natural, given our starting point. But it is inconsistent—when pretending to discuss matters comprised in this polarity—to foist upon the argument terms embedded in our *present* vantage-point, which stands *outside* the state we are trying to characterize. I have called this application to an earlier state of the features and terminology of our own "advanced" subject-object experience *logomorphism*. To find our way back would in truth amount to a kind of inner archeology, and could not be achieved without some transformation of the researcher's consciousness in parallel with the transformations we see in evidence in what remains to us of earlier cycles (comparatively late historical ones of course) in "outer" cultural artifacts. This is where I find Steiner's work illuminating.

JRW: So the devolutionists imply that, at the outset, or at least at the beginning of the remotest historical cycle, "spiritual states" occurred in individuals who were (quite paradoxically, in view of their devolutionary views) *more or less like ourselves*—that is, in individuals located in space and time essentially as we know it, who had sense organs and perceived an "outside" world essentially as we do, but one somehow so illuminated by spiritual reality that the subject did not come into such clear relief?

OB: This is the very nub of the error. "Subject" and "object" are only relative terms, entirely independent of content. It is easy enough for anyone to state abstractly that ultimately "I am the World, and the World is I," but "reality" may be a far better starting point. As Coleridge points out, there is a polar logic at work in all things (Steiner invoked Goethe, particularly his scientific writings, to make the same point). You must be able to *distinguish* the two sides (and their common boundary continually shifts) without *dividing* them. If you divide only, then you end up either as an esoteric Perennialist devolutionist, or as a crass materialist evolutionist. There are certainly elements of truth—and imposing truth—in both sides, but the *whole* truth is lost.

JRW: In *Saving the Appearances* you imply that we in fact must "make" the world; that our observed world in the past was "made for us" (and this in differing measure as time progressed). On the historical, or *macrocosmic*, level this could lead to a discussion of the move from an "enchanted" or mythopoeic consciousness, through our contemporary epistemological starting point, and on to the spiritually creative function of future human culture. On the individual or *microcosmic* level, you point out that, in a way, the nature and role of the faculty of imagination has now retreated to a pre-conscious position in the modern individual, whose much-touted "objectively clear" consciousness is in fact as determined by what now constitutes the imagination as were his allegedly gullible forbears by "external" imaginations of mythological form. This pre-conscious faculty you call *figuration*. This, raised into consciousness, you speak of as active *participation*, whereby separation between subject and object is overcome through direct, creative spiritual collaboration in the divine drama. This collaboration derives from the initiative of the individual *will* that can only realize itself through first facing the abyss of alienation from "externally" imposed principles, through *freely embracing*—in love— these same principles, but newly "created" in each moment by a moral imagination and moral intuition. As you say, before he moved into the astonishing esoteric material that characterized the last twenty years of his life, Steiner had presented his exposition of the epistemological foundations for such a view, especially in his *Philosophy of Freedom*, which he always referred to as far more important than the far-ranging details of his later lectures. He claimed that his epistemology represented the way back for modern man, but a way "back" by going forward.

OB: Yes. But to return to figuration. This process is like an unconscious imagination. Now, what I mean by conscious participation is our gradual taking over of the pre-conscious figuration process. This has to do also with the imagination, but an imagination at the conscious disposal of an *individual*. My goodness, the subject is quite complex! But Coleridge had a good handle on it. I tried to make some sense of it in my *What Coleridge Thought*. The point is that our very concepts of the most fundamental starting-points of discussion give evidence of the evolution of consciousness; how then can we pile them all up on the past?

JRW: Perhaps we can put it this way. One side looks at dissolution in the Absolute as the goal, and individualization as a fall; the other side sees the Absolute as well, but believes there to be a meaning in the individual: that the individual is in fact *the* meaning of the cosmic process. The rub seems to come with the role of the individual. In fact, without some precisions being made, it may seem that even the "individualists" want to end up at the same dissolution in the Absolute. But is such a dissolution that never crystallizes out individuals (or does so only *provisionally*) the same as one that arises from the conscious choice of individuals somehow fallen from the non-individual state? Does the *re-integrated* individual or ego not give at least some faint "pastel tint" to the Absolute when "fused, but not confused"?

OB: We're on the edge of the unthinkable here, you and I. You can't use

"individuality" or "ego" as a final criterion. Such terms signify different things during the overall process. And in any case, "ego" carries other connotations. Individuality becomes commensurate with the cosmos. (I think we must leave aside here the question of the Absolute.) This is true of the ego, but in using this term we are clear that where it enters in there is a *moral* issue. The obligation to become commensurate with the cosmos is certainly rather overwhelming!

JRW: What is the end-point? Perhaps it would make things clearer by beginning at the end.

OB: Excellent! Let us then be "preposterous"! Well, I suppose you'd have at one and the same time the maximum of both the individual and of the cosmic: the polarity of microcosm and macrocosm attains its maximum contrast and is then overcome.

JRW: You see, all this gives a profound metaphysical meaning to the discussion of time. Processes in time—history, the whole drama of individuation, if we want to risk a term that has such intractable Jungian overtones—these you are treating as *not* ultimately relative, but as having an ontological significance. And as for the individual that unfolds in time, along with the freedom that is its concomitant, you suggest that when and if it can return to the Absolute it somehow retains its identity?

OB: Ultimately for me, as for Steiner, freedom *is* the Absolute. We go through all this troublesome evolution to procure individual consciousness, and then cooperate freely with cosmic consciousness. "Ye shall be as gods" is a dangerous formulation, and highly elliptical, but it has its significance here.

JRW: Are you saying that the individual, exercising its freedom, can overcome the polarity it arose from, dissolve subject-and-object, bring things together again in a unitary state, while remaining individual? Can it accomplish this alone?

OB: I'm afraid such questions are beyond me. This coming-together, however, certainly cannot be only by virtue of the individual, but also by virtue of God, of the Godhead, of the Absolute. One cannot make the many necessary distinctions involved here in such a brief conversation. Certainly we need God to "become as gods"; otherwise we have fallen into the trap Satan set for Jesus Christ in the wilderness.

JRW: In the final analysis it seems that we are focused on the final significance of time, or perhaps of time and space and that point of final condensation we have been calling individuality.

OB: We can't use our concept of time here in the usual way. Time is so difficult to understand. We usually think of it as some kind of mathematically contrived system with elements of space brought in (clocks and so forth), as some kind of *measurement*. We have to have a different grasp of time to answer such a question. Space seems to derive from the non-sensible world, something relatively easy to

picture after one has become convinced of its existence; but time derives from something that I suppose we can only call *duration*.

JRW: That sounds a good deal like Guénon. But he speaks in terms of *possibility*; that is, that a world is deployed (this word is felt to somehow circumvent the issue of evolution) temporally in accord with a system of "compossibles," the rudiments of a world that exist in a pretemporal state—call it duration if you like. But he infers very different things from this than you do, for you center on the notions of individuality and freedom.

OB: If all manifest processes pre-exist as possibilities, or systems of these as "compossibles," where is there room for individuality and freedom? In the "possibility of impossibility," as Guénon somewhere puts it?

JRW: I believe this unique possibility Guénon reserves for what we call evil.

OB: It seems more suited to the possibility of freedom, though I wouldn't deny that freedom and evil are closely connected, very closely connected, indeed. Freedom, duration, and time are hard to grasp. We mathematize these notions and make them into abstractions.

JRW: Again, what is the end-point?

OB: Well, I think the New Jerusalem described in the New Testament is as good a description as any I could come up with. One thing is certain—we are in an evolutionary crisis right now… But you seem uncertain about what I am saying?

JRW: The stakes are high aren't they? If we opt for the evolutionary view, then what of traditional forms? It's one thing to discuss these matters: it's another to face life's trials with nothing but the promise of some glory of the individuality-to-come. What of the remnants of tradition that still surround us, and to which many sensitive spiritual seekers instinctively turn when they begin to see through the deceptions of the chaos that surrounds them? Have they no significance?

OB: Of course they do. We cannot decide anything about that in any case. There are many people and many needs. Tradition will be there (but undergoing change, howsoever you may wish to reconcile this apparent contradiction) as long as need be. Ultimately, traditions are inwardized—that's the crux. I don't think one can come to a clear understanding of this unless one sees it in the light of reincarnation.

JRW: But let's suppose you're right. Even so, the flimsy individual—your own flimsy individuality, if you'll pardon the presumption, but in your case… [*Barfield was 98 years old at the time.*]

OB: Indeed!

JRW: …the flimsy individual must seem shadowy indeed, even in the dying light of Tradition, especially as one confronts the last of life's trials.

OB: Of course. And I can understand the tendency to turn back to the past. I think it is, finally, a matter of one's own destiny. But in the long view I cannot doubt that what is so understandably sought for now in the past (or, as might be objected, in the "eternal" outside time and space, for which the "past" often seems to stand in Perennialist thought) will eventually be found to lie in the *future*, though "with a difference"— the very difference for which the whole process was set in motion! We only have this abyss to cross, this intersection of time and eternity, the horizontal and the vertical. And this is the Christian symbol *par excellence.*

JRW: This Christian image of the intersection at the center of the cross, is it so relevant to your view?

OB: Indeed it is. God became Man. The Incarnation of the Word is the *meaning* of human history. Christ was resurrected and the great process of the Redemption of Creation began. This is too complex a subject to go into lightly, and I, in any case, am not qualified to give the answers. But, ultimately, we are talking again here of the overcoming of the polarity of I and the World. Since the Incarnation, Passion, and Resurrection, I cannot see how the final meaning of the evolutionary dimension, the redemptive dimension, however difficult it may be to reconcile it with the Perennialist position, can be denied.

TWO POEMS

Ruth Asch

SOUL AND BODY (I)

I too, have seen the Sacred Hour fly—
or felt her shadow fall as light wings lifted,
a glimpse of haloed feet which had passed by…
Her absence, in a breath held—
a crystal shrine to call her—
shattered by the pressure of a sigh.
What had I seen, in those shrouded moments?
Who was it spoke, in the silent dark
where all the world I knew was white
with noise—a deluge swept,
turbulent, round about this ghostly Arc?
There was Immensity, into its bosom
I might have cast myself, had I known how—
and in its heart the question:
Love infinite asking vow for vow.
I paused…
Waiting for the perfect answer.
Found it not in my echoing brain
nor in the deepest rummage of my shallow, cluttered heart;
so sought it with a plea—
the artless child's refrain,
expecting every answer from the questioner again—
Self-searching did I from the Unknown part.

Beautiful was she, who hovered then and fled,
as though a living thread in His angelic floating train.
Her features, through the billowing mystery
movingly veiled, yet spoke like friends to me:
childhood Saints each had some presence there;
In her embrace, a spirit's, I was drowned,
as air too rarefied nascent soul to suffice;
she was, nor held, an attitude of prayer;
her eyes, most human, glowing charity…

Then, the daily world impatient grew
into this porous mind, and she was gone,
without the slightest trace, and yet I knew
the purest part of all my soul, was she.

Never more that blessing has returned.
No more do I now wait for it, and long…
Whether she or I the other spurned,
God knows.
    I would be urged
to think no longer of a failure past,
of the question none can answer and live on.
Cast off sad pretence of saintly strife,
yearning for a state forever gone.

Then shall I turn to my material self:
full blooded, sensual, carefree?
Play with her each day a double masque:
catching her mirrored wink
at the thoughts I dare to think;
smiling at the scarlet lips,
or the curve of breast and hips;
absorbed in sheer sensation,
and the full preoccupation
of how to be the wonder that is me?

But senses sate and starve over again;
and image is not person, we soon find.
A man unsouled echoes a hollow tree,
stark, sinister, stunted and doomed he;
So plucked flowers, gorgeous in decay,
in melting lines across the pavement stray:
women, from their conscience torn away.
My soul and body are one, and alive;
a marriage indissoluble, their faults—
but most, their selfish isolation—halts
the flow of sweet and sorrow where they strive
to be a whole harmonious, and pray.
Each only fulfilled when they both give;
I Am in both, and both for Him live.

SOUL AND BODY (II)

Never was there true un-fettering
between the ego and the doubt-filled dark.
I had once felt to lose oneself in God
was self-annihilation—but, then, stark
madness is to choose yourself a self,
mind-limited, obsessive to one goal—
or be besieged by voices fracturing
your own experience. To cast one's soul
into God's otherness is not to fall
into unconscious void—rather to launch
upon a sea of light, where we are held
by consciousness divine—Being more staunch
to our true nature than we'd hope to be;
and He will not forget, his love is all
the immanence which gives eternity.

His presence is itself the answer
to all the questions I do not quite know;
The missing feeling of true wanting
which should be there—never is quite so.
A consciousness which delights in others—
unhindered by the shy or greedy self—
glimpsed here through His living essence,
will be, in heaven, all our wealth.
To leave the prison-cell of self-deficient,
the bridge of evidence is strong though slim:
not to believe in a notion of myself
but to believe with my whole self in Him.

And where to find him—
when I must leave the altar,
or the moment of passion-peace is gone?
His face is in my brother,
who looks for Him, I hope, in me.
I find myself, forgetful in the other—
the ego, in Divine love, free.

ASH WEDNESDAY BLUES

Michael K. Kivinen

Imposition of ashes
Memento mori
Yes, I know
It's come to this:
Now you are here
A lifetime later
Alone in the stillness
Down at the crossroads
Where vertical and horizontal meet
In cruciform intersection of Spirit and matter
Recalling that the Infinite One,
Although illimitable and unlimited,
Came trailing glory
But clothed Himself in limitation and form
To be emptied
To be desiccated
To be tempted, tried, and lifted up
To exchange Being itself for being's cessation
To die like you will die
In godforsaken forsakenness
For you too have been pinned and limited
On a lower arc
Restricted by form and time
On your cross of heredity and condensation:
Your Gethsemane, Your Golgotha
On that unsightly hill on the outskirts of town
And just this side of the Abyss
Mud to dust
And kingdoms to rust
Will you cast off comfort and company?
Will you enter this wilderness alone?
Blinded by blistering daylight desert sands
And then shivering in dark night, chill and void
To spend forty days bereft of habit, confronted with
        compulsion and craving

Alone to face your soul
Startled, as if by a panhandling stranger
But even this bum in rags of dirty denim
With his greasy hair and boils
Bears the Image and Likeness of *Logos*
You'd never know it by the looks of him—
His scars and scabs, his poverty of speech
Might fool you into fear
Or frighten you into derision
But wait: He needs your mercy
Your succor
Thou art that shade
That shape is you
And he awaits you now
In the desert
Hurry! You'll find him there
So alone with wild beasts and unaware of angels
That even the Adversary would seem like a long-lost friend
If he tempted you there with crusty bakery bread
Made of freshly-gathered stones
With the promise of protection
With the kingdoms of this world
When he showed you his snakeskin boots
His serpentine dance moves
His flickering tongue
His way with words and his icy eyes
He might give you cigarettes and make you believe
That all the ladies loved him
Don't you realize that he's an elegant distraction?
Get that liar behind you, at least until the appointed hour
Go back to your soul, your Self
That's who needs you now
He needs your mercy
Your prayers
Your attention
Your contrition
Your sorrow
Your hope
He's been waiting in this desert for forty years
While you went wandering in some far country

Almost pissing away your inheritance
On lottery tickets, cigarillos,
Pepsi, potato chips, and *People* magazine
Until bringing back some costly souvenirs
To show your Father where you'd been
And beg for His mercy
And a few savory scraps of fatted calf
Before washing His feet with what's left of your hair
So let your soul sip silence from an alabaster jar
Splash soothing, cooling ointment
Over his thick, dark sores and pockmarked face
And remember that you
Are this dust
These sands
This wilderness;
That by becoming silence and looking with care
By getting to know yourself as you are known
Perhaps you will find
That even these mirages are pools of limitless Light.

Poet or Priest?

Romilo Knežević

*Previously published in *Poem: International English Language Quarterly 2* (2013)

AN LIVES IN HISTORY and he cannot help using historical means for creating relationships, either with God or with other men. One of the historical means *par excellence* for communication is, certainly, language. If we say, together with John Zizioulas, that man is a relational being, we have to go one step further and claim that man is a being of language. If the essence of man's relational existence is language, we are bound to elucidate the semantic of this language.

Rainer Maria Rilke's "transformation" of the visible into the invisible is operated by means of language. Man cannot save the visible unless he creates the language of the invisible, as Maurice Blanchot argues in *L'Espace Littéraire*.[1] I argue that the manual side of our acts represents solely external crust. According to Archimandrite Sophrony Sakharov, who was a priest

and an artist, the Eucharist is performed in the way it is, in order to keep in our mind as fully as possible Christ's deeds during His life amongst men. Sakharov writes that the priest who prepares himself for celebrating the Eucharist is obliged, according to his powers, to have in his mind and in his entire being[2] the meaning of Christ's redemptive journey on earth: "Let this mind be in you, which was also in Christ Jesus" (Philippians 2:5). A manual act acquires its full meaning only if taken together with the noetic attitude that follows it. One external act can have many different and even mutually excluding meanings depending on the thoughts that accompany it. So I fully agree with Jean-Louis Chrétien when he writes that manual praise presupposes speech:

> So there assuredly is an operative praise, a manual praise. *But it presupposes speech, as in any case its social character confirms, and it cannot be seen as its opposite.* St Augustine thinks of agricultural labour as dialogue with nature: "Human reason can in some degree speak with the nature of things."[3]

[1] Maurice Blanchot, *The Space of Literature* (University of Nebraska Press, 1989), 142. "If the metamorphosis of the visible into the invisible is our task, if it is the truth of conversion, then there is a point at which we see it through without losing it in the evanescence of 'extremely momentary' states… 'How,' says Rilke, in a text written in French, 'how could one sustain, how could one save the visible, if not by creating the language of absence, of the invisible?'"

[2] Archimandrite Sophrony Sakharov, *His Life is Mine* (Crestwood, NY: St. Vladimir's Seminary Press, 2001), 87.
[3] Jean-Louis Chrétien, *The Ark of Speech* (New York: Routledge, 2004), 144.

Nothing that we do only with our hands can be regarded as a genuine Eucharist. Man has to act with all his powers, corporeal and spiritual, undivided. In each of his human acts, his whole being ought to be focused and fully present; otherwise his actions are incomplete, feeble, and ambiguous.

If manual praise presupposes speech, it means that we have to look for the inner-noetic, language-related meaning of the Eucharist. According to the original Greek word εὐχαρ-ιστία,[4] as is well known, the Eucharist is the act of thanksgiving or expressing gratitude. Still, how can we establish the relation between human expression of gratitude to God and human creativity responsible for the transformation of the whole creation? In other words, what is the essence of thanksgiving? Jean-Louis Chrétien writes that to think is to thank.[5] We find exactly the same presumption in Heidegger:

> The Old English *thencan*, to think, and *thancian*, to thank, are closely related; the Old English noun for thought is *thanc* or *thonk*: a thought, a grateful thought, and the expression of such thought.[6]

I argue that *vice versa* is also the case; that *to thank is to think*. In this way we interpret thanksgiving more broadly and see that it encompasses human relation to the created world. In order to be genuinely creative, therefore, Eucharistic thanksgiving

ought to entail some sort of thinking.

However, I do not mean any kind of thinking, but the "thinking of being."[7] In the Eucharist we give thanks for all the gifts given to us by God, but first of all we are expressing thanks for the supreme gift: that each one of us is an absolutely unique person, created in the image of God, which means that we are beings endowed with *logos*. Here I argue that human capacity of *logos* is the power of thought. Nonetheless, I don't understand thinking as an operation of human being performed in a *vacuum*, that is, thinking as a result of human ipse-ity. If being was created out of nothing, it bears the characteristics of its Creator. This implies that being of the created world is *logos*-like, that it bears the resemblance to God the *Logos*. This view is expressed with particular emphasis in the works of Gerard Manley Hopkins:

> In the light of the Incarnation, for Hopkins even aesthetic experience is somehow Christened. In this light too, within the context of Duns Scotus' influence, Hopkins perceived nature to be Christically expressive. The Incarnate Word is the ultimate pattern and intelligibility of created being in its various and singular manifestations.[8]

[7] "The thinking of being is the primordial form of poeticizing." Martin Heidegger, *Off the Beaten Track* (Cambridge: Cambridge University Press, 2002), 247.

[8] Philip A. Ballinger, *The Poem as a Sacrament: The Theological Aesthetic of Gerard Manley Hopkins,* Louvain: Peeters Press / Grand Rapids, MI: W.B. Eerdmans, 2000), 234. A bit later in his work, Ballinger assesses that, according to Hopkins, "creation is Christic in its core" (240).

[4] See: *A Greek Patristic Lexicon,* ed. G.W.H. Lampe (Oxford: Clarendon Press, 2004), 579.
[5] Jean-Louis Chrétien, *The Ark of Speech*, 119.
[6] Martin Heidegger, *What is Called Thinking*, trans. J. Glen Gray (New York: HarperCollins Publishers, 2004), 139.

Although they don't use Christian terms with regard to their experience of the created world, one could argue that even secular writers such as James Joyce and Marcel Proust write about the enigmatic *essence* of matter or what Hopkins called the *inscape*.[9] Joyce, by virtue of his education very close to the Jesuit Hopkins, named this essence the *whatness* or *quidditas* of things, while Proust wrote about the *general essence of things*.[10] One could hardly deny the striking similarity between the *whatness, inscape,* or *general essence of things* with what Heidegger named the *gods*.[11] For Heidegger, the created world eventually—by being logosic or Christic, possessing the traits of the divine[12]—is an abyss of meaning and consequently the "most thought-provoking food for thought."[13]

The Eucharist, in order to represent authentic human creativity, ought to be a giving thanks which thinks of the potentially infinite reach of being. The true Eucharist is not simply an act of external piousness in which the priest offers the gifts to God. It is quite unclear from Zizioulas' work what the activity of the congregation should be in the Eucharist. One has the impression of a congregation's sheer passivity, as if only the priest, and not every man, has the vocation to be the priest of creation. Here, of course, I am not talking about the sacramental priesthood: which does not mean that this sort of priesthood is absolved from the necessity of thanking as thinking of the being. I am talking about the priesthood which is the gift given to every human being by virtue of the fact that he is a living being endowed with *logos*,[14] and that man's use of the capacity of *logos* has an immediate ontological impact on the whole creation. If this is the case, it should be observed that in Heidegger's concept of human creativity and, consequently, in his notion of the priesthood of man,[15] we find human agency. Heidegger's understanding of the (non-sacramental) Eucharistic act is close to the Christian mystical contemplation of the logos-like nature of creation:

> How can we give thanks for this endowment, the gift of being able to think what is most thought-provoking, more fittingly than by giving thought to the most thought-provoking? The supreme thanks, then, would be thinking? And the profoundest thanklessness, thoughtlessness? Real thanks, then, never consists in that we ourselves come

[9] Ibid., 236.

[10] James Joyce, *Stephen Hero*, ed. Theodore Spencer (New York: New Directions Press, 1944), 211–13; Marcel Proust, *Á la recherche du temps perdu: Á l'Ombre des jeunes filles en fleurs* (Paris: Gallimard, 1988), 24 and 182.

[11] Martin Heidegger, *Parmenides* (Bloomington and Indianapolis: Indiana University Press, 1992), 112.

[12] Ibid.

[13] Martin Heidegger, *What is Called Thinking* (Chicago: Henry Regnery Company, 1967), 143.

[14] "According to this determination, man is ζῷον λόγον ἔχον—the being that emerges from itself, emerges in such a way that in this emerging (φύσις), and for it, it has the word." Martin Heidegger, *Parmenides*, 68.

[15] Although Heidegger does not use the term "priesthood," I think it is quite adequate in this context.

bearing gifts, and merely repay gift *with gift*[16] (emphasis added). Pure thanks is rather that we simply think—think what is really and solely given, what is there to be thought.[17]

Neither the sacramental Eucharist nor the inner one can consist of physical acts only: they include a much more complex and demanding activity of human logos capacities. Can we, then, postulate that in the Eucharist thanksgiving which is thinking represents also both an interpretation and incantation of the essence of creation? If to *thank* is to *think*, if God's activity is apprehended as artistic and, subsequently, if the creation represents the "holy book," *liber naturae*[18] or the work of art, then this book can be read and interpreted solely by virtue of poetical means. Heidegger's view, that "The thinking of being is the primordial form of poeticizing,"[19] appears to lead to the conclusion that the creation is the work of art and that, logically, the only possible way to interpret it is poetical.

I have asked, nonetheless, if thanksgiving as thinking can be understood both as interpretation *and* incantation. Here, I confine myself to saying that incantation indicates the ontological relation between thinking of being and the being. To interpret the being is at the same time to incantate it, to renew it, to re-create it, and to liberate it from the consequences of fallenness. This is how I understand Heidegger's words: "The poeticizing essence of thought preserves the sway of the truth of being."[20]

If man is a language being, then it is by the very essence of discourse that he is in an ontological relation with the being of the created world. This is more so because the being itself is made of a speech-fabric. Chrétien explains this point, drawing on Paul Claudel:

Things must offer themselves to us so that we may in turn offer them by offering ourselves, and both of these offerings will be made possible by speech: "Created speech is that in which all created things are made such that they can be given to man."[21]

On the other hand, the innermost logic of human language is re-creative in its core. The syntax of human speech rebels against any form of given-ness and petrifaction. It requires, moreover, constant negation and deconstruction of the already-achieved and represents a vital invitation to absolute newness.

[16] Here one has the impression that Heidegger describes the priest carrying the gifts in the Eucharistic procession.
[17] Martin Heidegger, *What is Called Thinking*, 143.
[18] David Bentley Hart, *The Beauty of the Infinite* (Grand Rapids, MI / Cambridge, UK: William B. Eerdmans Publishing Company, 2003), 291.
[19] Martin Heidegger, *Off the Beaten Track* (Cambridge: Cambridge University Press, 2002), 247.
[20] Ibid., 247.
[21] Jean-Louis Chrétien, *The Ark of Speech*, 132. Compare: "In the word and as word the Being of beings is given in relation to the essence of man in such a way that the Being of beings, in virtue of this relation to man, lets man's essence emerge and lets it receive the determination that we call the Greek one" (Martin Heidegger, *Parmenides*, 68).

The nature of human speech is Christic in the sense that it follows the same path of Golgothian dying and resurrection. In his remarkable book *Towards a Christian Poetics*, Michael Edwards claims that:

> The constitution of language itself, even prior to writing, suggests a latent propensity for the contradicting and re-saying of the fallen fact. Verbs, for example, reach out of the-world-as-given in tenses and moods such as the conditional, the subjunctive, the optative; a "syntax of counter-factuality and contingency" opens to a realm of possibility, of liberating hypothesis. And if the way we make language attests to an obscure, partly conscious desire to elaborate it as a strategy of renewal, it is already just such a strategy, as Mallarmé argues, in its simplest, least mediated form. The word "fleur," when said, or when pronounced and heard in the mind's ear, is big with metaphysical activity. Language, however little we ask of it, is already a process of death and resurrection, and is thereby related to the process fundamental to everything.[22]

It seems that, unless we accept the broader connotation of the notion of thanksgiving as thinking of being, it is impossible to comprehend the Eucharist as a genuine human creativity related to the transformation of the created world. In this sense, the human priesthood should be understood as connoting man's poetical vocation. The meaning of both vocations can be derived only from the nature of man as a discourse-and-relation-creating being. Man is a priest of creation only if he is a poet of creation.

Nonetheless, is Christianity able to espouse such a centauric symbiosis? It seems that the vocations of the priest and that of the poet are rather in conflict than in concord. G.M. Hopkins himself provided many reasons for questioning the compatibility of these two vocations: "He clearly struggled with their co-existence in his life and never achieved a peaceful synthesis of the two."[23]

Sakharov went through almost the same crisis when his "passion" for painting came into conflict with the newly-born and extremely strong desire for prayer:

> The beauty of the world around combined with the miracle of the dawning vision enthralled me. But in my art I tried to sense, beyond the visible reality, the invisible, timeless essence which afforded me moments of exquisite delight. However, the hour came when increasing mindfulness of death entered into outright conflict with my passion for painting. The struggle was neither brief nor easy. I became a sort of a two-dimensional battleground: the grace of mindfulness of death did not descend to earth level but summoned me to higher spheres. Art began to define itself as something lofty, transcending the material plane, in its finest achievements

---

[22] Michael Edwards, *Towards a Christian Poetics* (Grand Rapids, MI: William B. Eerdmans Publishing Company, 1984), 146–47.

[23] Philip A. Ballinger, *The Poem as a Sacrament*, 63.

touching on eternity. All this travail was in vain: the disparity was too obvious, and in the end *prayer* won.[24]

I have already claimed that I do not understand art or artistic creativity solely as a cultural phenomenon. I use art only as an example to outline the main traits of artistic creativity, which is the activity aspiring to create out of nothing, and to use its principles in the context of the human relation to God and the rest of creation.

Sakharov's view on art as a cultural phenomenon was mostly negative. Nevertheless, there are tokens in Sakharov's work that attest to the fact that he was also aware of the broader meaning of artistic creativity and that he had special admiration for it. Perhaps the most obvious example is from Sakharov's homilies to the monks and the nuns of his monastery, and his exclamation; "O, how I wish that all of you could become poets! Without the creative inspiration it is difficult to live even one day according to Christian standards."[25]

[24] Archimandrite Sophrony (Sakharov), *We Shall See Him as He is* (Tolleshunt Knights, UK: The Stavropegic Monastery of St John the Baptist, 2004), 15.

[25] Arhimandrite Sofronii, *Duhovniye Besedi Tom 1* (Esseks/Moskva: Svyato-Yoanno-Predtechenskii monastir / Izdatelstvo "Palomnik," 2003), 259.

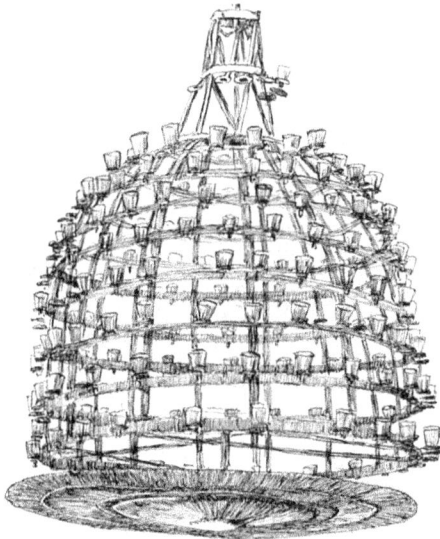

THREE POEMS

John Slater

APOCALYPSE

In the next room
the new
Sonic Boom
Alarm Clock is
ticking and
set to detonate.

*

'canary in the mind'
lot with cars
gone leaving
a desolate beach
of gravel
chemical reek of
cornfields spread
with ketchup and
cream-soda
hosed off
cannery walls.

*

Not "undead"—
fresh
naked bodies
nosedive up
through cracked
sandy earth
into the radiant
golden cloud
into the folds
of the slate-

blue veil
that falls over
all
as the crowd
starts to murmur
and the house-
lights brighten.

THAT NATURE IS A HER

Cloud-
Built thoroughfare:

                                 whitewash |

                            ín long | lashes

Delightfully

                    squeezed |

                                bonfire

                                        gone
                                          dark

                          blots   out
                I   all
But vastness blurs and | beats level. Enough!

                Across my foundering
                  beam
          the residuary
                flash,

This   poor
                  diamond.

SO TINY A TRICKLE OF SÓNG

So tiny a trickle of sóng-
                              found

            behind or
       left
Anywhere in the súnlight.

With white strokes

the wheat-acre   underneath
                              breaks out
The ear in milk, lush
                    poppies

Bud shelling or broad-shed

Foam-tuft
             . . .   within

       the longing

       And after that off the bough

Ultimate Reality and the Matter of John Cowper Powys

Michael Sauter

"Philosophy collects and articulates ideas which are haunting the ether at specific times and which are sensed by artists, who, like animals, foretell by their behavior the earthquake that is on the way. So, art and philosophy, in their different ways, are in touch with 'Being,' which is the way things are in their ultimate reality, rather than the way they appear to our myopic self-obsessed contemporary vision."[†]

~ Dom Mark Patrick Hederman, OSB

[†]Mark Patrick Hederman, *The Haunted Inkwell: Art and Our Future* (Dublin: Columba Press, 2001)

E CAREFUL OF STREETS named "Fourth."

Thomas Merton, as is well known, had a famous vision at Fourth and Walnut in Louisville that showed him "ultimate reality" and he awoke "from a dream of separateness, of spurious self-isolation." The gestation of this present short piece began on the corner of 4th and Madison in Washington DC, just outside the National Gallery of Art (good sign!), when the monk/writer quoted above told me to "make a case for Powys someday" in the way that he, in his book, made the case for artists like Rilke, Wole Solinka, Iris Murdock, James Joyce, and others. The "case" here refers to demonstrating the relevance of certain philosophical and poetic outliers to the renewal of Catholic imagination. John Cowper Powys, in his threefold significance—as a most unique theological interlocutor with C.S. Lewis, Maritain, Berdyaev, and Niebuhr; as a prophetic critic of the expanding cult of science; and as an anarchist herald of the spiritual properties of matter—is more than well deserving of a hearing.

John Cowper Powys (1872–1963), the Wales-loving English novelist, lecturer, philosopher, literary critic, and poet, though still relatively unknown, does have his strictly *literary* admirers, and important ones at that. Author of over twenty novels, a number of them among the most lengthy in the English language, Henry Miller, for one, said of him that, "To encounter Powys is to arrive at the very fount of creation"; and no less a figure than George Steiner listed Powys's fiction as the only fiction in English on par with Dostoevsky. Robertson Davies,

Angus Wilson, Iris Murdoch, J. B. Priestley, and Philip Larkin, who referred to Powys as a "gigantic mythopoeic literary volcano," were also admirers. He has his political admirers, too. It is a noteworthy sign in politically confused times like these that Powys's thoughts regarding the coming "State-Despotism" gets two chapters in David Goodway's excellent book on left-libertarian thought (Good things in that direction lie!), *Anarchist Seeds Beneath the Snow*, alongside other political "honeybees of the invisible" such as William Morris, Oscar Wilde, George Orwell, and Aldous Huxley.[1] Dorothy Day, had she read Powys, would have undoubtedly found a kindred spirit.

But what of religion?

Son of a Dorset vicar and eldest of 11 children, Powys *knew his Bible*. And we know from his writings that he was also very well read in Church history. He was certainly one of the most well-read people in England of his generation. A liberal of sorts (a witness for the defense in the obscenity trial of James Joyce's novel *Ulysses*) and personally unsuccessful at marriage, he debated Bertrand Russell in 1929 on "Modern Marriage" in New York City in favor of traditional marriage, almost echoing Chesterton (whom he admired) in making the case for monogamous marriage as the more *imaginative* of the two contrasting visions being debated. He also wrote a short, decent book called

The Religion of a Sceptic (1925), making the case for what he called "imaginative religion" as a *tertium quid* of sorts in the "age-old controversy between the modernists and the fundamentalists in religion." A Christ-haunted individual, his monumental *Autobiography* (1934) depicts a years-long tug of war with the Catholic faith; and yet, in the main, he could also be classified as anti-Catholic: a perceived emphasis on dogma to the exclusion of vision and abuse of authority distanced him. Like the poet Coventry Patmore and others, Powys was concerned mostly about religious *perception* and, relatively early in his career, wrote a book about what we can and cannot discern when all the faculties of the soul are working in harmony to form what he called "The Complex Vision." A Trappist monk of my acquaintance said of the book, "I have never seen such powers of introspection." Regarding his stance on official Christendom as a whole, what Merton said of Blake need also be said of Powys:

> He saw official Christendom as a narrowing of vision, a foreclosure of experience and of future expansion, a locking up and securing of the doors of perception. He substituted for it a Christianity of openness, of total vision, a faith which dialectically embraces both extremes, not seeking to establish order in life by shutting off a little corner of chaos and subjecting it to laws and to police, but moving freely between dialectical poles in a wild chaos, integrating sacred vision, in and through the experience of fallenness, as the only locus of creativity and redemption. Blake, in other

---

[1] David Goodway, *Anarchist Seeds beneath the Snow: Left-Libertarian Thought and British Writers from William Morris to Colin Ward* (London: PM Press, 2011).

words, calls for a "whole new form of theological understanding."[2]

Ditto that, word for word, for Powys. In fact, on comparisons between Blake and Powys alone, there is enough to fill, according to one Blake scholar, "a doctoral thesis, if not several!"[3] Certainly he calls for a "whole new form of theological understanding."

In theology proper, Powys engaged often and fascinatingly—especially in his books *Mortal Strife* (1942), *Dostoevsky* (1947), and *Rabelais* (1948)—with the thought of C. S. Lewis, Maritain, Berdyaev, and Reinhold Niebuhr in particular. Of the four, Berdyaev fascinated him the most. A small sample of his reaction to them shows him reflecting on where they come up short:

> What unites Maritain and Lewis and Professor Niebuhr in an indissoluble Security-Pact is their attempt to regard the deep, dark, black holes in the cosmogonic firmament through which blow the free anarchistic winds of interstellar space as contrivances of the Devil. Berdyaev struggles desperately to let in a little Russian air and allow a few patches of virgin forest to remain inside the Park Walls; but he plays the necromancer too easily, to my thinking, with that serpent-rod of his, the tricky syllables "spirit" and "spiritual." Yes, for them all there must be a disparagement of ordinary history,

a "lower estimate" of ordinary goodness, and a reduction of ordinary wisdom.[4]

Now it is no doubt possible that a small sample might come across as flippant. But I suggest that his style and intelligence is better described as "Rabelaisian" in the deadly serious meaning of that term:

> It is extraordinary how few among even the most devoted readers of Rabelais seem to take literally, and accept as the essential truth about him, what he says in his own Prologue concerning Socrates and the grotesque exteriors of the Sileni-Boxes of precious ointment. Why haven't we learnt from Don Quixote and Sancho, from Mrs. Quickly and Falstaff, from Dickens and Chaplin, the fact that humour at its homeliest can be the very "charity of St. Paul in a Comic Mask"?[5]

Having read everything I've ever found of Berdyaev translated into English (with a decent amount of Maritain and Lewis thrown in), I can attest that his engagement through the course of these books is as informed as it is nuanced, eye-opening, and absolutely necessary.

Powys spent decades on the lecture circuit in Britain and America. (He noted that Catholics related to him and understood him more than Protestants: might be the humor.) And reports of people in the audience swooning or literally passing out during his lectures are legion, such was his claimed ability to *inhabit the*

[2] Thomas Merton, *The Literary Essays of Thomas Merton,* Br. Patrick Hart, ed. (New York: New Directions Books, 1960), 6.

[3] Michael Grenfell, "John Cowper Powys and William Blake," http://www.michaelgrenfell.co.uk/literature/john-cowper-powys-and-william-blake/.

[4] John Cowper Powys, *Rabelais* (London: Bodley Head, 1948), 378.

[5] Ibid., 8.

atmosphere and inmost thoughts of the writers he loved. The exhilaration of reading Powys engage with the best theologians of his time is tied to this, almost psychic, ability of his. In reading him, you sense that you are reading Maritain, for example, engaged by the incarnate sensibility and wisdom of Homer, Aristophanes, Rabelais, Goethe, Cervantes, Dostoevsky, and Shakespeare, individually, or, more commonly and magically, all of them combined!

Powys claimed that there was a commonsensical, prophetic, earth-born, humorous, magical, "equality-of-all-souls" tradition of sorts in this literary pantheon of his. And he argued in many of his works that the sum total of the wisdom in these books called explicitly, in our time, for a "transfer of reverence," away from the "religious reverence for sex and our sexual reverence for religion" and back to "the life for which is was intended," and that, until we do so, we shall never be able to "argue about good and evil and right and wrong without lapsing into moral, if not into physical, burnings and torturings." Good advice, that. Powys further suggested that this "transfer of reverence" back to life, which might also constitute the mythical marriage of the East and the West yearned for by many, was to take its cues not from the utterances of some New Age Eastern yogi but, in fact, in alignment with the prophecy of the sixth-century Welsh poet Taliesin, who later became the mythic hero and companion to King Arthur, and what Taliesin intimated about "the African secret." Look, he seems to suggest, for dawn to break in that direction!

Powys placed his hope in Africa because of the similarity of the syntax of many African languages (and the Welsh language!) to Aramaic and, hence, the real poetry of the Gospel, but also, at least in part, because he saw the East getting overrun in a similar way as the West had been overrun by the horrifying spirit of analysis-for-the-sake-of-analysis, which was Baconian Science. His anti-vivisection novel, *Morwyn or The Vengeance of God* (1937), which features a Dantean trip to the Underworld, was exclusively dedicated to this theme: "The moral atmosphere of Hell, its power of concentration, its lack of distraction, its indifference to right and wrong, its ghastly fatalism are all conditions that lend themselves to scientific progress."[6] Torquemada and Calvin as well as an Everyman (a stand-in for millions of this type) sort of research scientist were put in the lowest circle of hell and, in the mouth of Socrates, speaking of the history of science, Powys states:

I didn't mind it so much in what I understand you call your Middle Ages; for though, very learned in the works of one of my pupil's disciples, an industrious student of Nature, they still put the Human Conscience and the difference between Good and Evil in the forefront of their doctrines. But a dreadful person—I believe he belonged to your remote island—whose patronymic was Bacon, turned up, and since his time everything went wrong. The soul of a wise man, the conscience of a good man, became no longer the test of the

[6] John C. Powys, *Morwyn, or The Vengeance of God* (London: Village Press, 1976), 142.

purpose of the System-of-Things. And it gets worse and worse.[7]

During his career, from beginning to end, Powys was a resolute drawer of comparisons between "The Twin Gods of Religion and Science," as in "the religious bigot of Predestination and the scientific bigot of Determinism," "Religion killing for the truth of the past and Science killing for the truth of the future," and so forth. There was something in the spirit of a scientific curiosity, ceaselessly taught in our schools to praise, that horrified him. It didn't just risk "killing the cat." It literally killed millions upon millions of cats, dogs, and monkeys in research laboratories. And worse, this spirit, said Powys, led inexorably to the "unsexing" of ourselves, "mixed up good and evil," was completely tone-deaf to the "ironic method" of Socrates, and was counterproductive to any "ennobling of the human character, enriching of the human mind and any real philosophical wisdom." He ultimately suggested that, "Only the baa-ing ewe lambs of our research inquisitors fail to miss the religious dogmatism, the illiberal fanaticism, the unphilosophic inhumanity of those aspects of modern science wherein all the old blood-sacrifices and all the old dark sorceries and secrecies have come back!"[8] Such was his output on this theme that one group of Powys scholars, in summing up his *oeuvre*, writes: "We dare single out one of Powys's thoughts as a symbolic projection of his philosophy: that the triumph of science, like the triumph of the Nazis, will mark the era of the totalitarian anthill and that only elderly people's long experience on the earth stands between us and a biological catastrophe."[9]

To some, undoubtedly, that will seem like an overstatement. To many, however, it is candor.

Now in order to understand the visceral as well as intellectual horror Powys felt in the presence of the animating spirit of Baconian science, which claimed to put "nature on the rack," it is said that Powys daily prayed with hands outstretched for God to *physically* intervene in stopping the work of vivisectors. It is imperative, then, to understand his feelings and insights into the, as it were, raw material or "ultimate reality" of science itself: matter. To Powys, matter was most definitely not "dead" (anything but), and in *The Complex Vision* he actually has a chapter about his own perceptions regarding matter, entitled "The Illusion of Dead Matter." One thinks of Novalis, another intrepid explorer into the spiritual properties of matter: "The mound became a cloud of dust—and through the cloud I saw the glorified face of my beloved."[10] And, as Michael Martin says of Goethe, "he was committed to countering Cartesian and Newtonian approaches which treat matter as a thing at hand, something to be used, a methodology analogous to rape."[11]

7 Ibid., 248.
8 John Cowper Powys, *Obstinate Cymric* (London: Village Press, 1973), 180.
9 Radco Adamovick, "At Last: John Cowper Powys," http://www.powys-nnion.net/Powys/LettrePowysienne/ALJCP.pdf.
10 Novalis, "Hymns to the Night." https://logopoeia.com/novalis/hymns.html
11 Michael Martin, *The Submerged Reality: Sophiology and the Turn to a Poetic Metaphysics* (Kettering, OH: Angelico Press, 2015), 111.

Powys's own spirituality, inspired directly by Goethe, was grounded in what Goethe's *Faust* referred to as the "invocation of the four," as the four elements were always the focus of Powys's extraordinary gifts of perception:

> There is a subtle humility to be found in this giving yourself up to the elements and in thus taking your share in the long patience of the animal and vegetable entities that draw their sustenance from the elements, that harmonizes very curiously with some of the deepest psychological secrets in both Tao-ism and Christianity where these ways of life are taken experimentally and not systematically.[12]

For Powys, personality was absolutely central; and for him all matter, including objects as simple as doorknobs, possesses some residual, if fleeting, elements of feeling and personality. Like Goethe, and against Baconian, Cartesian, and Newtonian approaches, Powys had an "erotic metaphysics" that could not remain indifferent to personality, to means and ends. In his strange and prophetic book of his life-philosophy, *In Spite of: A Philosophy for Everyman* (1953), he even preached an erotic gesture of sorts (he saw himself as something of a magician), which was an embracing of projected consciousness, though still connected with the body, with select groupings of matter we find around us, as a form of evolutionary ascent. And it was matter, for Powys, and not a descent of the Muse, which was the very stuff of the upwelling creative genius responsible for those works of fiction and creative philosophy in which he immersed himself. He suggested, regarding Dostoevsky and Rabelais, that, in their inspirations, "so far from becoming in the remotest degree 'godlike' they become on the contrary the impersonal mediums of Inert Matter."[13] The Eucharist, I submit, suggests the same.

So there we are. John Cowper Powys was *sui generis*. There is literally too much to say—he, himself had too much too say—but introduced to us he must be. Nicholas Berdyaev said that each Christian receives a special genius from the Spirit, and John Cowper Powys followed his like he composed many of his sentences: on and on and on. But a genius he undoubtedly was. The Orthodox theologian Olivier Clement once stated that the 19th Century, "with a few notable exceptions," was an age of spiritual slumber when "Christianity degenerated into moralism," and I think there is not much evidence that the 20th was much better. It is conceivable, then, that we may have corporately lost a sense for how to read works of genius. We are so used to being able to get a hold on, and control, works that we can, figuratively, stand above that we have lost a sense for the gift of seeking understanding. It is in that spirit that I put forth, in paraphrase, in regard to Powys what T. S. Eliot offered in regard to Simone Weil: "We must simply expose ourselves to the personality of a [man] of genius."

---

[12] Powys, *Obstinate Cymric*, 171.

[13] John Cowper Powys, *Dostoevsky* (New York: Haskell House, 1973), 38.

THREE POEMS

Charles Upton

VOICE OF THE ANTICHRIST

Inside my own body, my will is law: I leave nothing to chance.
Neither priest's black book nor pale human morality hold the power
To bend the fixed rod of my course.
I purchase and put on the fiery image that gives me power over the stars;
I admire myself, when day is done, in the frozen mirror of cocaine.
Circumstances fall to me, and jobs, and sales, and deals;
I reap my profits, invest them in global empire,
Because man is made to conquer the future, to cut his way, by pure self-will
To the galaxies of his ultimate form.
The findings of impartial research reveal my word to have been inevitable
        from the beginning;
The future is assured to my flesh;
No other lives in my image. I cut out the impostors
With knives, with military interventions,
With judiciously placed rumors, with massive transfers of capital;
I grip the wheel of the stock exchange, aiming for target center with the
Weapon of mobile assets; the pirates of my right and my left hands
Come from all the finest mafias and universities…
I am without rival. The sentimentalized face of God the Father
I have limited to residual pockets of sub-colonial darkness in rural backwaters;
The Virgin, too, is abducted by my warriors and bound to my desire;
Night and Silence have no power over my
Hard, undying light.

MESSIAH

Who are we
Who were born at the end?
Are we the best, or the worst of men?
Latter-day saints,
Or demons in human form?
What bitter, medicinal juice
Was destined to be twisted out of us

That we came here to breathe, and walk
In this time
And at this place?

The warped mirror of this world
Caught your image, Messiah,
And nailed it to a blackened rock
Under a stream of barren, coursing thought.
That was the hook that dragged and lifted me from my sport
In the shining ocean of Beginning.

But now, as the air grows thin
And the bedrock wavers
You show yourself again
Through the fading veils
Of earth
And thought—
In the crypt of this secret chapel
Are milk and honey hid.

So lift dust and nugget, and pan them out.
Gold in the sack remembers the motherlode;
Honey in the pot remembers the mountain where it was born.
As sky sleeps, inverted, on the face of the ocean,
So now ocean rises, bodily,
And turns to sky entire.

SACRED RED AND BLUE DAYS

I

Bound
Under the sterile eyes of wolves;

Mothered to ash
In the ovens of time's end;

Born standing again
Under the new dispensation
On the paved earth—

Have we returned again to this battlefield
Only to recite the
Litany of our crimes?

Better to be
Featureless clay
In the hands of the Potter, fabricator
Of the Earth to come.

II

Knowledge is cash and cash is time
To sit in the concentric circles of your bloat
Hedged by psychic minefields,
The simple archaic alphabet of fear and desire…
Lesson One: you have escaped the consequences;
Lesson Two: the consequences are still there,
Fear looking inward, toward the altar of Love,
Desire facing outward, toward the altar of Fea…

My finger is on your shoulder,
Slight, constant pressure, easily bearable—
Except that I require that you simply turn
And face me now: Don't worry,
You have already been released;
I am only reading the record backwards,
As every death most certainly requires.

III

Whatever this contemporary river is I must have missed it,
Having chosen for my "rendezvous with history"
Five years in a river of burning slag.
In that glowing bath, the chain that linked me to passing time
Melted completely away, except for these nuggets of ore
I am presently feeding
                              To that same burning river:
Fire fed to fire;
Chaos to chaos;
Repentance to sanctity;
Error to truth.

IV

Where were these hills, and where was I
When the thread was lost that bound us?
Is that why they now dream, heavy with sorrow
Locked in the cavern of the Earth-killer,
Where the footprint of the Secret Adam, the primordial Human Form,
    is rubbed out—
He of whom the Subtle Folk
Were the radiant elementals?
Is that why the buried skull of him is now filled
With the sniggering voices
Of the Jinn?

Only when man is Man again
Will these hills return from exile;
Only God's eye
Looking out through the eye of Man can see them as they are:
Gardens beneath which rivers flow,
Arteries of vitality and of truth.

V

If it is true that we will now fight all the old wars in reverse,
It is also true that, though loser now wins and winner loses,
The prize is not the same: death is life now, and life, death.

And the meanings of life and death, these too are reversed:
What we struggled all our lives for is simply what we were handed to
    begin with,
While the hand we were dealt by merciless fate, the very thing we fled from
Is perfected work now, image of the heart's desire.

VI

The struggle with the angel—it changes so fast.
He escaped through my grappling hands like
Snakes of quicksilver. Transmuted into lead,
I lived through the desert of his absence.
If I could fix the angel in stance, in breath,
In finest will, in subtlest practice, O my soul,

You know I would do it. I am nothing but the
Smoke of his gestures. God's is the light;
And his, the solid hand; and mine, the shadow.

VII

Stopped for interrogation at the apocalypse border,
All past history rolling in behind me, piling up
For the final burning—
All the treasures and the junk of karma,
Farewells that pierce the heart, then abandon it,
The vastness of endings,
The heavy weight of rotten fruit,
Huge decadence and fall.

We are the ones condemned to have a memory.
We stand and watch the death of the Sun
On an Aztec altar off the Farallones
Bleeding into the lap of Night…

Death is a completed planet in a distant sky, receding
Into the frigid bodiless blue of the Future
A whiff of liquid nitrogen, acrid and cold…
It's way past time for it, no question about it.
Whatever is capable of death
Was never capable of life, so let the purification proceed;
Let the fire grow fat on all the
Dross in my soul;
Let death fall from me
Like a city.

VIII

That Word who left the mouth of God
To propagate himself in waves of Enlightenment
Comes back robed in his corpses, at cycle's end,
All the fates that tried to name him
Now the facets of a single crystal.
And, crossing the military border, his mirror-image,
The Serpent of Subtle Continuity, brother to the only Word God ever said
Between the gold and the lead

—He who establishes duration by the fixed burning-glass of present time—
Stands up. He wraps the risen Word around him in ascending spiral
Like an incandescent nerve,
Awakening him to One Form, One Man
Forged from myriad tiny unawakened beings
Curling to clotted dense sleep for
Fear of Fire. All change joins
Tail to mouth around
The Jacob's Ladder,
The diamond axis
Of our dance.

IX

Your vision fills the waking world
Like the Sun. The Moon
(as Yeats said) will then be inside us,
"The Antithetical Tincture,"
The true aristocracy, where each man
(as Blake said) is "King & Priest
In his own house,"
Each of us a great Sun Door
In the solitude of his own soul—
Translucent crystal,
Window of fixed air—
Where the whole past is redeemed,
Returns effortlessly to the
Center of its own delight,
The empty mirror, the great expanse of
Conditionless space,
Prajñaparamita, she who is Space Herself when
Rung like a bell, clearing a path
For the Lightningbolt, the clapper that strikes
Between the root and the crown
Of anything.
His ministers shine out from the central
Void of his kingship
In twelve-thousand rays.

If he were brought into this world
With a heart and a face
He would be, precisely,
You yourself.

THREE POEMS

Emi Shigeno

CALLING

beyond a windowpane
edges fogged

past unrelenting gale
and at its mercy

swirling cloud of flakes
and even beyond

the oblivious, gay, and unbeheld
memory that never was

stands bare, an oak
save a leaf spinning wild

solemn and still
roots spread deep

bearing silently
the weight of snow

wearing a gaze tender
over sorrow

a bare foot hastily
kisses the white

melting what was and
in its place a sting

reaches the marrow
now abiding

and the kettle screams
on the stove

demanding my presence
my bare foot

and smothered with steam
the outstretched limbs

into faint lines
smeared on glass

BACKYARD PENTECOST

Bereft

of sky's immensity
overgrown with trees

I yield to be engulfed
by a kindred squall,
unforcasted,
save by the shades
of longed for honesty

The boughs gave way to gales
shedding stale leaves and
bits of paper
In its aftermath, tongues of fire
separated from the setting sun
two millenniums and a forest away, and

came to rest on a limb
or leaf whose face was wet—
until snuffed out by the dark

Whispers slid off
the veins and into
the blue mist, lingering

on my lips

DECEMBER

time of year when
I'm drawn to seek refuge in

an old B&W photo from
an attic stained with rain

teamed horses infusing
the air with manure

rainbows carved into
toadstools on rotting logs

earth graced with lacy
skeletons of leaves

weathered skin of an old
farmer rising before dawn

moss on my abode
decomposing in the fog

TWO POEMS

S. L. Davidson

THE ABSENT GOD

I am, but know not what it is to be,
I am not you, therefore I look at you,
I keep you in my gaze, you sweet enigma,
And for a moment, empty of myself,

Explore that art that keeps you in my eye,
Uninvented, except by the naked void,
Whose silence alone can comment on itself,
Speaking volumes of nothing, all about you,

Unaided, our dreams, scattered through the night,
Will dissipate in darkness to darkness' gain
And I will never have to tell you this thing
About the absent God, which I cannot explain,

You know it already, you who reduce me to colours
And stretch my body out like a spectrum of light.

NO MAN'S HAND

As you move your hand, I do not want
To know what blunders terrorize the race,
I don't care what kills me, and I bless
Bullets that sleep in boxes as we play,

Who had grown so serious on politics,
And the potential falling down of heavy rain,
That we almost forgot to lose ourselves together
In gardens left to us by the happy dead,

You keep your laughter with you unconcealed,
Now no-one is a god for you to fear,
You blunted the fangs of the world with a brittle brush
Painting mushroom clouds into my dreams,

And I wondered where my fears had gone, and then
I ceased to wonder that, and simply wondered

Prologue

Simone Weil
(1909–1943)

H E ENTERED my room and said: "You miserable wretch, you who understand nothing and know nothing— come with me and I will teach you of things you do not know." I followed him.

He led me into a church. It was new and ugly. He led me before the altar and said: "Kneel." I told him: "I have not yet been baptized." He said: "Fall down on your knees before this place, with love, as before the place where truth exists." I obeyed.

He led me out, and up to a garret from whose open window one could see the whole town, some wooden scaffoldings, and the river where boats were being unloaded. He made me sit.

We were alone. He spoke. Now and then somebody else would come in, join in the conversation, then go away.

It was no longer winter, It was not yet spring. The trees' branches were bare, without buds, in a cold air full of sunshine.

The light grew, dazzled, and then faded, and the stars and the moon shone through the window. Then again the dawn arose.

Sometimes he would be silent and take some bread from a cupboard, and we shared it. That bread truly had the taste of bread. I never found that taste again.

He poured for me and for himself wine which tasted of the sun and of the soil upon which this city was built.

Sometimes we lay down on the wooden floor of the garret, and the sweetness of sleep descended over me. Then I arose and drank the light of the sun.

He had promised me teaching, but he taught me nothing. We talked about all sorts of things, ramblingly, in the way of old friends.

One day he said to me, "Go away at once." I fell to my knees, embraced him by the legs, and begged him not to chase me away. But he threw me out to the stairs. I descended them without awareness, as if my heart were in pieces. I walked through the streets. Then I realized I didn't know where this house was.

I have never again tried to find it. I understood that he had come for me in error. My place is not in this garret. It is anywhere, in a prison cell, in some bourgeois parlor full of knick-knacks and red plush, in a waiting-room at a station. Anywhere at all, but not in that garret.

I cannot help myself sometimes from repeating, in fear and remorse, a little of what he said to me. How do I to know that I remember it correctly? He is not here to tell me.

I know well he doesn't love me. How could he love me? And yet there is something deep inside me, a point of myself, which cannot help think- ing, with fear and trembling, that per- haps, in spite of everything, he does love me.

Translated by Michael Martin

Jerusalem, Temple Steps, James J. Tissot, c.1895

A Spring Ending for the Winter's Tale

Fr. Jonathan Tobias

IN SHAKESPEARE's play, *A Winter's Tale*, the bad guy comes to a pretty good end. He should have ended up tragically, like Macbeth. But, for some reason, the play turns out to be a comedy instead of a tragedy.

Not that he deserves it. King Leontes of Sicilia acts monstrously. He accuses his best friend and his wife of adultery. He scorns his baby daughter as illegitimate and orders her to be abandoned in the wilderness. He imprisons his wife Hermione and prosecutes her so cruelly that their son, Mamillius, dies of a broken heart.

Now if this were a classic Greek tragedy—like Euripides' *Medea*—the story would stop right there. The main character would die at the point of greatest suffering that he had brought on himself because of his *hubris*: but then he would be made noble and heroic by that suffering. The hero would have to suffer to pacify the angry gods. His nobility would serve to "improve" the rest of the city—and mankind—with the quality of the hero's death and sacrifice.

And I should note here that Greek tragedies were only interested in the suffering of aristocrats: the suffering of the poor is given no attention,

because, as Nietzsche liked to ask, what does it really matter?

It is remarkable how so many people (especially some religious writers) understand the crucifixion of Christ in just this way—as a Greek tragedy. Christ suffered, and in that suffering—so they say—He became a hero, maybe even the very best of heroes, who gives meaning and hope to human life. Therefore (so they say) the Resurrection is an "unnecessary" addition to the real, essential story.

So, in this line of thinking, the story of Jesus is good enough if it ends right at the Cross. The Resurrection is only a fairy-tale happy ending, like "and they lived happily ever after." You don't need the Resurrection—again, so they say—because the really important stuff, the hero and tragedy stuff, has already been accomplished at the tragedy of the Cross. In fact, it doesn't even matter if anything in the story actually happened, because it is enough, in Greek tragedy, for a myth to give us a heroic story to improve our humanity.

But a story that ends at the Cross is not good enough at all. In fact, such an unfinished story misses the main point of the Gospel, and ends up making it meaningless. There can be no Cross without the Resurrection.

There is Golgotha and there is the descent into Hell: that much is a story that the world is too familiar with. The world expects tragedy and finds it difficult, if not impossible, to think outside this script.

But the whole point of the Gospel is that this tragic cycle of the world is finally broken. The meaning of the Cross is that the Resurrection has ended the fateful necessity of suffering and tragedy. The Crucifixion was not the sacrifice of a hero to soothe an enraged god: instead, it was an offering of infinite peace, and the start of a universal beautification. God the Father most certainly did not take out His wrath upon Jesus on the Cross: He, and the Son, and the Spirit worked to pour out divine life at the darkest point of tragic death. There was no wrath at all: there was only, instead, the restoration of full communion between God and Man, and the new definition of sin and death as empty meaninglessness (that is why "weeping and gnashing of teeth" are now located in the outer darkness, the place where only fools and apostates go, no longer in the proper place of man).

Without Easter, the Cross would have only confirmed our worst suspicions that violence and power always win out, as in *Medea,* and history belongs only to the aristocrats. With Easter, however, everything shines. And the tears of a poor fisherman like Peter actually mean something.

The meek, after all, really do inherit the earth. The Cross alone would not have accomplished this. But the Cross with the Resurrection? Indeed, all things now are possible.

Shakespeare is known to have let Easter shine in much of his work, and *The Winter's Tale* is no exception. The term, "Winter's Tale," refers to a story that is told in front of a glowing hearth on a long winter's evening: "Pray you sit by us and tell 's a tale," Queen Hermione says to her doomed son Mamillius, who replies, "A sad tale's best for winter. I have one of sprites and goblins." And believe you me, the next few acts are full of this, but of the far worse human variety, in the form of a demonized husband, father, and king.

The great bard was never one to resist a pun when one shows up to play. The clever joke of the play is that toward the end, Spring breaks into the Winter tale. Leontes is downright evil at the beginning. But his heart breaks over the next sixteen years. He visits his wife's grave repeatedly, and he mourns her with bitter tears. He suffers the loss of his baby girl and the early death of his son. He regrets his rash betrayal of his true friend. So much does he grieve that his friend, Cleomenes, tries to re-direct him: "Sir, you have done enough, and have performed a saintlike sorrow. No fault could you make which you have not redeemed—indeed, paid down more penitence than done trespass." But Leontes, now exorcized by the hard passage of sixteen years, disagrees: "Whilst I remember her and her virtues, I cannot forget my blemishes in them, and so still think of the wrong I did myself, which was so much that heirless it hath made my kingdom and destroyed the sweet'st companion that e'er man bred his hopes out of."

There, right there, is repentance, worthy of any Prodigal, or any King David.

But life, in its post-Resurrection complexity, has a way of renewing the dead past for repentant monsters. Providence is just like this, so unpredictable, so much a happy riddle. It turns out that Leontes' baby girl was not abandoned after all, but was put in the care of a family of poor shepherds.

It is intriguing that it was amongst the shepherds that the ice starts to melt in *The Winter's Tale*. In their pastoral setting, these meek, unfamous, very a-political folk have the imagination to work out an ending that differs radically from the expected tragic script. Recall that "shepherd" in Greek is "*poimén*," which in turn is a term deeply related to poem and poet—shepherding and poetry are together joined in the working out of imagination into art.

And I am here to tell you that *it is only Easter that makes possible the rise of comic imagination in the context of tragedy*. The Resurrection makes poetry to rise in the night of mourning.

Unbelievably, the girl Perdita, now sixteen, falls in love with Florizel, the princely son of Leontes' old friend, and ends up in her father's palace. "Unbelievably," because no tragedy-addicted cynic would ever accept such nonsense. But sometimes, many times in fact, the invisible is made visible, the impossible is made possible.

There, right there, is a meeting unlooked for, but miraculously gained.

"Then you have lost a sight which was to be seen, cannot be spoken of," says a witness of this glad reunion. "There might you have beheld one joy crown another, so and in such manner that it seemed sorrow wept to take leave of them, for their joy waded in tears."

For father and daughter, it is a reunion after death in Act Five that wipes away the tragic weight of the first four Acts. It is genetically related to the overwhelming Grace-charged words at the eu-catastrophe of Dante's *Purgatorio*: "*Guardaci ben! Ben son, ben son Beatrice . . . non sapei tu che qui è l'uom felice?*" (xxx. 73, 75).[1]

The Resurrection of Jesus makes all reunion possible, and thus, the comic imagination of Spring. Just *because* the grave was found empty on the first Sunday morning means that your grave sorrow too will be emptied one day, when you see your family and friends again in an unending day, where there will be no separation or loss. Then you too will understand the meaning of "joy that wades in tears."

There is a final reunion in *The Winter's Tale* that is too beautiful, too good to relate here. You'll have to read it yourself. But I will give you a hint with these words of Paulina at the end—she is the true heroine of this almost unbelievable play:

It is required you do awake your faith... Music, awake her! 'Tis time. Descend. Be stone no more. Approach. Strike all that look upon with marvel.

Yes, by all means, approach the stone of the tomb with marvel. For Pascha is the reason of the Cross. Spring ends the Winter's tale. Tragedy is over: the Happy Ending is only just begun.

---

[1] "Look at me! I am Beatrice, I am! . . . Did you not know that people here are happy?"

REGENERATION

Henry Vaughan
(1621–1695)

A Ward, and still in bonds, one day
        I stole abroad;
It was high spring, and all the way
      Primros'd and hung with shade;
    Yet, was it frost within,
        And surly winds
Blasted my infant buds, and sinne
      Like Clouds eclips'd my mind.

2.

Storm'd thus; I straight perceiv'd my spring
        Mere stage, and show,
My walke a monstrous, mountain'd thing,
      Rough-cast with Rocks and snow;
    And as a Pilgrims Eye,
        Far from reliefe,
Measures the melancholy skye,
      Then drops and rains for griefe,

3.

So sigh'd I upwards still, at last
        'Twixt steps, and falls
I reach'd the pinnacle, where plac'd
    I found a paire of scales;
    I tooke them up and layd
        In th'one late paines;
The other smoake and pleasures weigh'd,
      But prov'd the heavier grains;

4.

With that, some cryed, *Away*; straight I
                    Obey'd, and led
Full East, a faire, fresh field could spy;
                    Some called it, *Jacobs Bed*;
A Virgin-soile, which no
                    Rude feet ere trod,
Where (since he stept there,) only go
                    Prophets, and friends of God.

5.

Here, I repos'd; but scarse well set,
                    A grove descryed
Of stately height, whose branches met
                    And mixt on every side;
I entred, and once in
                    (Amaz'd to see't,)
Found all was chang'd, and a new spring
                    Did all my senses greet;

6.

The unthrift Sunne shot vitall gold
                    A thousand peeces,
And heaven its azure did unfold,
                    Checqur'd with snowy fleeces,
The aire was all in spice
                    And every bush
A garland wore; Thus fed my Eyes,
                    But all the Eare lay hush.

7.

Only a little Fountain lent
          Some use for Eares,
And on the dumbe shades language spent
          The Musick of her teares;
        I drew her neere, and found
          The Cisterne full
Of divers stones, some bright, and round,
        Others ill-shap'd, and dull.

8.

The first (pray marke,) as quick as light
          Danc'd through the floud,
But, th'last more heavy then the night,
        Nail'd to the Center stood;
        I wonder'd much, but tyr'd
          At last with thought,
My restless Eye that still desir'd
        As strange an object brought;

9.

It was a banke of flowers, where I descried
          (Though 'twas midday,)
Some fast asleepe, others broad-eyed
        And taking in the Ray,
        Here musing long, I heard
          A rushing wind
Which still increas'd, but whence it stirr'd
        No where I could not find;

10.

I turn'd me round, and to each shade
    Dispatch'd an Eye,
To see, if any leafe had made
   Least motion, or Reply,
   But while I listning sought
    My mind to ease
By knowing, where 'twas, or where not,
   It whispered; *Where I please.*

Lord, then said I, *on me one breath,*
And let me die before my death!

Cant. chap. 5. ver. 17
Arise O North, and come thou South-wind, and blow
upon my garden, that the spices thereof may flow out.

Contributors

Ruth Asch's book of poems, *Reflections*, debuted in 2009. Her work has appeared in literary journals such as *Ghazal Page, Peacock Journal, Mediterranean Poetry, Haiku Journal, Classical Poets Society*, and is anthologized by *Sonnet, Mother's Milk, Realistic Poetry* and *Aid to the Church in Need*.

Isak Bond is a teacher and the author of the poetry collection *The Sacred Spontaneity of Nakedness* (2013).

Laura Hennig Cabral is a life-long Catholic deeply inspired by the mysticism of the Church, the order of the natural world, and the perfection of God. Her work reflects her explorations on the relationships between the three.

Elias Crim studied classics at the University of California (Berkeley) and has worked in book and magazine publishing for most of his career. He is a contributor to the American Scholar, Front Porch Republic, and the New Urbs blog at the American Conservative. He is the founder and publisher at Solidarity Hall, a national blog focused on community renewal.

S. L. Davidson is a Scottish poet living in the west of England. His poetry deals with metaphysical themes, spiritual traditions, love, the sweep of history (including our own), and the plight of refugees, particularly that of the Kurds.

Devan Meade DeCicco is a speech pathologist and writer living in upstate New York with his wife and three children. A graduate of the University at Buffalo Poetics Program, he most recently blogs at *inalium.wordpress.com*.

Tyler DeLong lives in northern Michigan with his wife and four children. He spends his time with his family in the forest at their small homestead, toiling in woodcraft, reading, and putting thoughts down on paper.

Katie Hartsock's first book of poems, *Bed of Impatiens* (Able Muse Press, 2016), contains a sequence inspired by Augustine's *Confessions*, written in the voice of the saint. She is an assistant professor of English at Oakland University (Michigan).

Michael K. Kivinen is the married father of two young adults. He works as an addiction therapist and teaches college psychology courses as an adjunct instructor. In September 2015, after almost forty years in a distant country, he returned to the Catholic Church.

Romilo Knežević is a monk of the Serbian monastery Hilandar on Mount Athos, Greece, and also Doctor of Theology and Philosophy from Oxford. In his PhD thesis, *Homo Theurgos: Freedom according to John Zizioulas and Nikolai Berdyaev*

(November 2016), he argues that traditional asceticism is not the only path towards saintliness, but that this could be also achieved through artistic creativity. Romilo currently holds a post-doctoral position at the Philosophy Faculty, Catholic University of Paris. He is also a multi-awarded documentary filmmaker (*See You in the Obituary*, 1995), author, and poet.

Scot F. Martin works in the construction industry and as a freelance writer and previously taught English to teenagers for over fifteen years. His publishing credits include work in *Stand*, *Ignatian Solidarity Network*, and *Flourish*.

Philippa Martyr is a writer, researcher, historian, and occasional academic. She lives in Perth, Western Australia.

Jonathan McCormack labors to depict the invisible spiritual realities that war for the throne of our heart. "I wish to affirm the soul-savaging horror of life along with the half mad belief that, in the midst of this terrible pain, there is a God who aches to take us in His arms and wipe away every heart-sick tear."

Sebastián Montiel is professor of mathematics at the University of Granada. He is the author of *Curves and Surfaces* (American Mathematical Soc., 2009) and more than forty scientific articles in his field. In addition to his work in mathematics, Montiel has translated into Spanish works by Charles Péguy, John Milbank, Fabrice Hadjadj, and authored various essays of theology.

Novalis (Georg Philipp Friedrich Freiherr von Hardenberg, 1772–1801) was one of most important of the German Romantics.

Aaron Riches is a joint faculty member of the Instituto de Filosofía Edith Stein and the Instituto de Teología Lumen Gentium in Granada, Spain, where he teaches theology at the Seminario Mayor San Cecilio. He is the author of *Ecce Homo: On the Divine Unity of Christ* (Eerdmans, 2016).

Michael Sauter manages the retreat houses at the Trappist Abbey of the Genesee in upstate New York. He also serves as Director of Catholic Campus Ministry at SUNY Geneseo and adjuncts there in Humanities and Philosophy. Mike is married, has four children, and raises goats and chickens.

Therese Schroeder-Sheker, harpist, singer, educator, and clinician, made her Carnegie Hall debut in 1980 and is a Sony and Celestial Harmonies recording artist. She founded and pioneered the palliative medical field of music-thanatology and The Chalice of Repose Project. She publishes frequently on contemplative musicianship, music-thanatology, and the women mystics.

Emi Shigeno grew up in Japan where she practiced medicine. She currently lives in Pennsylvania, practicing various forms of art as a spiritual discipline and insatiable necessity.

John Slater has published three books of poems, *Surpassing Pleasure*, a first collection; *The Tangled Braid: Ninety-*

Nine Poems by Hafiz of Shiraz, a co-translation; and most recently a chapbook, *Lean*. Originally from the Toronto area, since 2000 he has lived as a Cistercian monk in upstate New York.

Tom Sturch is a husband and father in Tampa, Florida. He keeps a private practice in landscape architecture and writes poetry as a means of documenting creation as it is, simply as it means, violently as it shatters his poorly-constructed abstractions, and happily alongside its gardener making all things new. Other poems of Tom's may be found in *St. Katherine Review*, *Gargoyle Magazine*, and *Relief Journal*.

Fr. Jonathan Tobias is a priest of the American Carpatho-Russian Orthodox Diocese in Pittsburgh, Pennsylvania. He teaches Pastoral Theology at the diocesan Christ the Saviour Seminary in Johnstown, PA. A father and grandfather, he has been married to his best friend and confidante, Marsha, for over 35 years.

Charles Upton has been a Sufi for 29 years. He has published nineteen books, mostly on metaphysics and social criticism. In 2013 he invented the Covenants Initiative, an international movement of Muslims to defend persecuted Christians. His most recent book is *What Poets Used to Know* (Angelico Press/Sophia Perennis, 2016).

Francis Valentine is a farmer and laborer. This is his first publication.

Henry Vaughan (1621–1695), one of the Metaphysical Poets, was a Welsh Paracelsian physician as well as the identical twin of the Anglican priest and alchemist Thomas Vaughan.

Simone Weil (1909–1943), who was called by Albert Camus "the only great spirit of our times," was one of the most important Christian philosophers and mystics of the twentieth century.

R. Bratten Weiss works as an eco-grower and a lecturer in English literature. She has co-authored two novels and published poems in several venues. She lives with her family in eastern Ohio.

James R. Wetmore established the publishing company Sophia Perennis in 1995, and subsequently several other imprints, and now also serves as co-director of Angelico Press. He has edited and contributed translations to *The Collected Works of René Guénon*, new editions of the visions of Anne Catherine Emmerich, as also of the writings of Valentin Tomberg.

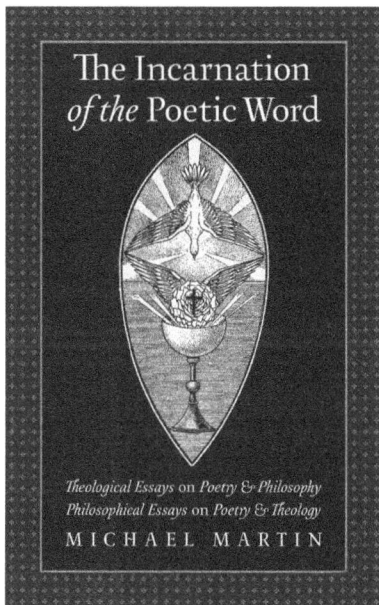

The Incarnation of the Poetic Word

Theological Essays on Poetry & Philosophy • Philosophical Essays on Poetry & Theology

MICHAEL MARTIN

In *The Incarnation of the Poetic Word*, Michael Martin brings together the worlds of theology, philosophy, and literary studies through the introduction of *agapeic* criticism, a method of inquiry characterized by reverence and attention, exploring what truly lives in the written word.

158 pages • 978-1-62138-239-3 (paper): $17.95/£15.00 • 978-1-62138-240-9 (cloth): $28.00/£23.00

"Michael Martin is one of those rare modern scholars who allows his speculative, artistic, and imaginative gifts to enliven and enrich his scholarship without any sacrifice of rigor."
— DAVID BENTLEY HART, author of *The Experience of God* and *Atheist Delusions*

"Michael Martin is a poet, a theologian, and a person of philosophical inclination—all of these roles diversely, and all of them communicating with each other in his rich writings. This, his plurivocal vocation, is given expression in *The Incarnation of the Poetic Word*."
— WILLIAM DESMOND, Katholieke Universiteit Leuven, Belgium; Villanova University, USA

"With its persuasive emphasis on recovering the contemplative, Michael Martin's *The Incarnation of the Poetic Word*, by turns prophetic, rapt, practical, and delightfully irreverent, plays adroitly at the frontiers of literature, philosophy, and theology—all in a poetic idiom. Martin's is a manifestly original voice that calls unabashedly for a posture of wonder, gratitude, and attention."
— JENNIFER NEWSOME MARTIN, University of Notre Dame

"Michael Martin's *The Incarnation of the Poetic Word* is a glimpse at the vision of one of the most exciting and creative scholars of our age. These are essays in phenomenology and criticism, but for me they are much more about cultivating the habits of intellect and affect that will leave us open, make us receptive, to the shining-out of Wisdom in the world around us. Martin summons us to move from the fist-clenched management of knowledge-production to the open-palmed receptivity that shares in Sophia's generative light."
— KEVIN L. HUGHES, Villanova University

"In Michael Martin's *The Incarnation of the Poetic Word*, we encounter a uniquely Sophianic confluence of philosophy, theology, and poetry, not as objects of study, but as transparent, so that we can see as if for the first time what shines through them. Savor this challenging and valuable book."
— ARTHUR VERSLUIS, author of *Theosophia* and *Wisdom's Children*

"The world needs Michael Martin's *The Incarnation of the Poetic Word*; it is a transformational work of rare artistry, intelligence, prayerfulness, and depth."
— THERESE SCHROEDER-SHEKER, The Chalice of Repose Project

MICHAEL MARTIN is a poet, professor, and musician, and lives on a small organic farm with his wife and nine children. He is also the author of a poetry chapbook, *The Book of Creatures* (Franciscan University of Steubenville, 2014), and a work of literary criticism, *Literature and the Encounter with God in Post-Reformation England* (Ashgate, 2014). His *The Submerged Reality: Sophiology and the Turn to Poetic Theology* was published by Angelico Press in 2015.

What Poets Used to Know
Poetics • Mythopoesis • Metaphysics
CHARLES UPTON

From the days of the first shamans, through Homer, Dante, the traditional ballads, Rumi, Blake, Emily Dickinson and Lew Welch, poetry has been rooted in metaphysics. In *What Poets Used To Know: Poetics, Mythopoesis, Metaphysics*, Charles Upton presents poetry both as a set of contemplative techniques and as a key to the accumulated lore hoard of the human race. If *The ABC of Reading* had been written not by Ezra Pound but by Owen Barfield or René Guénon or Robert Graves, it might have looked something like this. What *Poets Used To Know* does what it can to restore poetry to its original theurgic function: the concentrated expression of human and spiritual truth.

210 pages • 978-1-59731-171-7 (paper): $17.95/£15.00 • 978-1-59731-172-4 (cloth): $25.00/£20.50

"Dear Readers: Enter this book slowly, in the condition of awe, because it is a burning bush of recollection and transmission. Over decades, the poet Charles Upton has paid blood for an astonishingly sacramental and integrated artistry. His voice is movingly disarmed yet fierce. The author knows, cherishes and cultivates the linguistic and symbolic worlds of which he speaks. This volume consists of 19 meditative essays and a moving appendix by Jennifer Doane Upton on sublimity. Poets and musicians, theologians and philosophers, teachers and physicians, liturgists, gardeners and lovers need each and every page of this bright ship. In a world where self-knowledge is rare, fragmentation is the norm, and corporate and cultural spin abound, the truth source of *What Poets Used to Know: Poetics; Mythopoesis; Metaphysics* faithfully delivers a masterpiece. It is a joy to recommend it whole-heartedly."
— Harpist and singer **THERESE SCHROEDER-SHEKER**, The Chalice of Repose Project

"In *What Poets Used to Know*, Charles Upton initiates the reader into a kingdom long thought dead: the metaphysics of poetry. Standing in the lineage of the great Sufi poets, of Blake, of folk lyric, and of the Beats, Upton speaks with prophetic voice, a voice of one crying in the wilderness. For this poet 'poetry can be numbered among the final reverberations within the soul of God's creative act,' and it is to this act that he seeks to awaken our humanity, a humanity more and more entombed in the crystal coffin of postmodernity. To attentively read *What Poets Used to Know* is to enter an expansive, generous, and moral imagination; to learn again what it means to be fully human."
— **MICHAEL MARTIN**, author of *Meditations in Times of Wonder*

CHARLES UPTON, born in San Francisco, California in 1948, is a poet (a protégée of the Beats), a veteran of the peace movement, an activist, and a lifelong student of metaphysics and world religions. His entire formal education, from nursery school through high school, was provided by the Catholic Church. He has published four books of poetry and sixteen in the genres of metaphysics, mythopoetic exegesis, spiritual psychology, Islam, Sufism, and "metaphysics and social criticism." He is co-editor of *The Covenants of the Prophet Muhammad with the Christians of the World* by Dr. John Andrew Morrow (Angelico, 2013), and conceiver of the Covenants Initiative based on it, an international movement of Muslims to protect persecuted Christians.

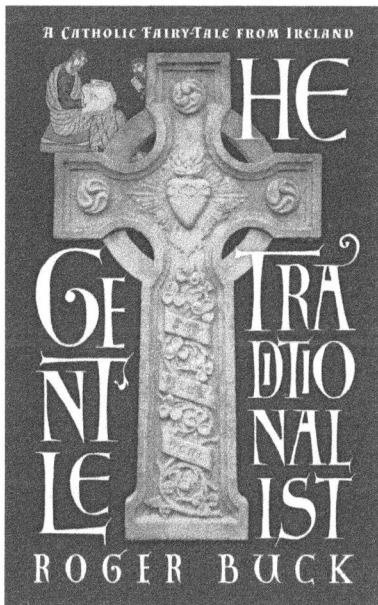

The Gentle Traditionalist
A Catholic Fairy-tale from Ireland
ROGER BUCK

Geoffrey has a problem. All his life he's lived according to "sensible" sceptical, secular values. Then, his true love left him for a New Age community in Scotland. But it gets worse: now she wants to be a traditional Catholic nun! Geoffrey is bewildered, angry, lost. Until, one Valentine's Day in Ireland, he meets a mysterious guide — the Gentle Traditionalist. Together they commence a most unusual dialogue of ideas concerning:

- The Real Nature of the Church: A Supernatural Mystery
- The Crisis in Catholicism today: the Loss of Tradition
- The New Age Movement
- Catholic Ireland
- Why Secularism gets away with murder
- The Heart of the Gospel

Both whimsical and serious, the dialogue in this book offers a probing exploration of the Catholic Mystery, Christendom, and the crisis of the West today. Join us for a very special Valentine's Day when Geoffrey's barren, rational world gets turned upside down....

194 pages • 978-1-62138-157-0 (paper): $14.95/£10.50 • 978-1-62138-158-7 (cloth): $24.95/£17.50

"This is one of the most unusual books I've ever read. It's a spiritual journey, a romance and a quest; a reflection on history and a discourse on faith and tradition; a fable and a meditation about place and location ... written throughout with passion and engagement, with a touching and deep-seated love for Ireland."
— MARY KENNY, author of *Goodbye to Catholic Ireland* and *Crown and Shamrock*

"Roger Buck in *The Gentle Traditionalist* employs the age-old genre of the Socratic Dialogue to examine that which would prefer not to be examined — the Western secular 'religion' that has come to define the society under which we in the so-called 'developed' world all live. As brilliant a guide for the perplexed as this age is capable of producing."
— CHARLES COULOMBE, author of *Puritan's Empire* and *Everyman Today Call Rome*

"*The Gentle Traditionalist* is a book with a 'strange magic,' like unto the Ireland it loves and mourns. With unforgettable images and a wry sense of humor, Buck unfolds a tale of whimsical fantasy, melancholy realism, and supernatural joy, ever so gently exposing the intolerance and incoherence of the New Secular Religion.... Buck's deftly-reasoned post-modern apologetic for full-blooded Catholicism will be salutary for those who are still wandering and for those already arrived in port."
— PETER KWASNIEWSKI, Wyoming Catholic College; author of *Resurgent in the Midst of Crisis*

"Writing with great wisdom, insight, and a most warm sense of humor, Roger Buck offers us a contemplation of the religious predicaments of our time in the spirit of Chesterton and Belloc. He takes on everything — from the reforms of Vatican II to the New Age, from the postmodern religion of science to the fallout from agnostic ennui — in a charming (and disarming) manner sure to delight readers already participant in Christian tradition, and to prove at least intriguing to those who are not. It is a wonderful book." — MICHAEL MARTIN, author of *The Submerged Reality: Sophiology and the Turn to a Poetic Metaphysics*

ROGER BUCK is a Catholic convert, who once resided at Findhorn, Scotland — probably the most renowned New Age community in the world. He is also the author of *Cor Jesu Sacratissimum* (Angelico Press, 2016) and a traditional Catholic website of the same name. He is very happily married and lives in the rural northwest of Ireland.

The Dream-Child's Progress
And Other Essays
DAVID BENTLEY HART

B y turns champion of the Christian difference and voice of dissent; friend to Moley and Water Rat and scourge to those of scientistic bent—these are but a few of the many guises of David Bentley Hart, whose books, essays, and reviews over the past twenty years have established him as one of America's foremost theologians, critics, and men of letters.

Few have escaped Hart's withering scrutiny, as he has exploded comfortable attitudes of believers and unbelievers alike. Here he turns his vital, and at times acerbic, pen to matters of truly high import: books and authors—and in so doing ranges far and wide across our intellectual landscape. Writing on everything from Alice to Zen, here are meditations on culture, theology, and politics; on words, sports, and nature.

Disarming, insightful, illuminating—and often wickedly funny—the essays in *The Dream-Child's Progress* give evidence of the great gift we have in Hart: a Christian intellectual engaging our world with warmth, candor, and clarity—but most of all, with charity.

358 pages • 978-1-62138-247-8 (paper): $24.95/£20.50 • 978-1-62138-249-2 (cloth): $35.00/£28.50

"David Bentley Hart's advocacy of remote literary treasures and lingering cultural mysteries will surely do much to offset the terrible reputation our universe must enjoy among the inhabitants of other dimensions. No more successful cosmic sales-pitch could be imagined."
— JOHN MILBANK, University of Nottingham

"David Hart is a national treasure. Like an ecologist lovingly displaying the beauty of a rare plant, or pinpointing where to find the real contribution of, or cure for, an invasive shrub, Hart masterfully guides us into the many ways in which humans attempt to express the intricacy and mystery of reality."
— MATTHEW LEVERING, Mundelein Seminary, University of St. Mary of the Lake

"A journey through the mind of David Bentley Hart is always a great and glorious adventure no superlative can describe and no summary encapsulate. Perhaps, then, the highest praise one can lavish on *The Dream Child's Progress* is to say it is not altogether unlike another journey undertaken with the guidance of Hart's beloved Lewis Carroll: it gets curiouser and curiouser with each wonderful essay."
— MICHAEL HANBY, Pontifical John Paul II Institute for Studies on Marriage and Family, Catholic University of America

"David Bentley Hart is an indispensable voice—brilliant, learned, arch, and pitiless. This far-ranging collection is quintessential Hart, by turns provocative and hilarious. I learn something unexpected from nearly every essay."
— KYLE HARPER, University of Oklahoma

"This volume is a nest holding many fine jewels. Once again, Hart has shown that he is the best writer on religion (and all things attendant) in America today."
— CONOR CUNNINGHAM, University of Nottingham

DAVID BENTLEY HART is currently a fellow of the Notre Dame Institute of Advanced Study, and the author of *The Beauty of the Infinite* and *The Experience of God*, among many other books.

The Chain
A Story of Faith Seeking Understanding
ANNA RIST

Reaching back into the previous century, *The Chain* tells with insight and humour the story of marital and other vicissitudes of an English Catholic family in a period marked by WWII and its aftermath: the breakup of the British Empire and passing of hegemony to America; the Second Vatican Council; and the social and educational developments of the mid-twentieth century.

This is the setting for the playing out of the great—arguably the greatest—theme of the conflict between Original Sin passed down through the generations and Grace communicated through the sacraments of the Church. Through vibrantly embodied characters, the reader is invited to enter into souls struggling—with varying outcomes—at an ever-shifting line demarcating Tradition and Modernity. The effect is cathartic.

The novel is neither didactic nor a surreptitious manual of doctrine, but is instead a carefully orchestrated, realistic story full of symbolism and resonances that speak to its time as also to our time, but beyond them to all times.

358 pages • 978-1-62138-259-1 (paper): $17.95/£15.00 • 978-1-62138-260-7 (cloth): $25.00/£21.00

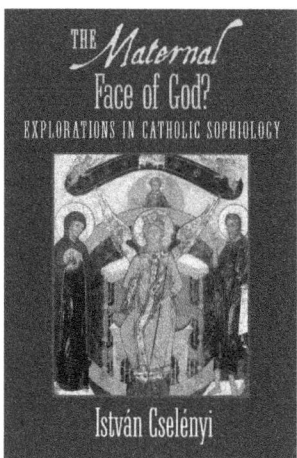

The Maternal Face of God?
Explorations in Catholic Sophiology
ISTVÁN CSELÉNYI

Until relatively recently, sophiology was almost entirely ignored by Western theologians. The modern West learned about sophiology from the Russians, the influence of which is palpable in the theological aesthetics of Hans Urs von Balthasar and in the Mariology of Louis Bouyer, to name only the most obvious examples. And yet, as this book shows, sophiology is at its core a Western phenomenon—and perhaps ironically, it was originally a Protestant phenomenon, as its fountainhead is the Silesian Lutheran cobbler Jakob Boehme. Indeed, Fr. Cselényi argues that Boehme's sophiology provides Catholic (and Orthodox) theology with a courageous and vigorous Mariology, a gift that has been for the most part left unopened.

It is only in the last decade or so that sophiology as such has been taken up with any theological gravitas in the West. Throughout his book, in addition to offering insight into the work of "canonical" sophiologists such as Boehme and the Russians, the author also investigates previously unexplored avenues of sophiological insight in ontotheology, in phenomenology, in the Fathers, and in Scholasticism.

234 pages • 978-1-62138-242-3 (paper): $17.95/£14.50 • 978-1-62138-243-0 (cloth): $28.00/£22.50

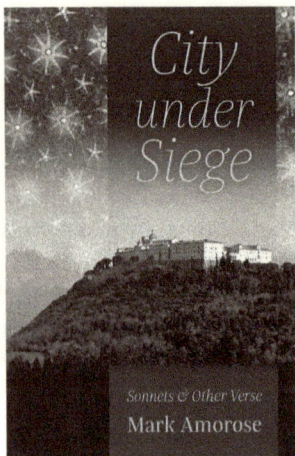

City under Siege
Sonnets and Other Verse
MARK AMOROSE

"In *City under Siege*, poet Mark Amorose ranges widely across Western history. In poem after poem of elegant formality (Amorose is a master of the Italian sonnet), the reader is taken on a journey from the pre-Christian world through biblical times, on to the high noon of medieval Christendom, and finally, through a flawed Reformation, Enlightenment, and Romanticism, to the spiritual wastelands of modernity. Amorose praises creation, the Catholic Church, Mary, angels, saints, and martyrs—his sonnet on English martyr Robert Southwell is magnificent; and he condemns reductive scientism, soulless commercialism, self-serving relativism, and widespread violations of the Church's teachings on sexuality. *City under Siege* is contemporary Catholic poetry at its finest. And it is an heroic defense of the City of God, a city now under siege, yet against which, in the end, no force can ever prevail." — DAVID MIDDLETON, Poet-in-Residence Emeritus, Nicholls State University

"Mark Amorose, a master of the sonnet and epigram, is a rare poet, one who overcomes poetry's most difficult challenge: religious poems. In his book's title, *City under Siege*, Amorose hints that America's culture is collapsing and its faith failing, while poetry saves our social and spiritual challenges with the help of God. Like the passionate Gerard Manley Hopkins, Amorose also writes poems with richly rhyming verse, a love of nature, and the wisdom of the gospels. Christians of every denomination should read this book and pass it on to friends and neighbors, to be further inspired by the author's art." — PAUL LAKE, poetry editor, *First Things*

84 pages • 978-1-62138-271-3 (paper): $14.95/£12.50

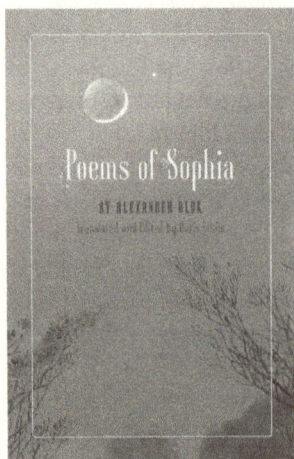

Poems of Sophia
ALEXANDER BLOK
Translated and Edited by Boris Jakim

Alexander Blok (1880–1921) is the greatest Russian poet after Pushkin and perhaps the greatest poet of the twentieth century in any language. This volume consists of translations of three collections of Blok's verse: *Ante Lucem* (1898–1900), *Verses about the Beautiful Lady* (1901–1902), and *Crossroads* (1902–1904). These poems describe Blok's visions of Sophia, the Beautiful Lady, who appeared to him at the end of the nineteenth century and the beginning of the twentieth. Sophia is the mysterious feminine principle behind all creation; Blok calls her the Mysterious Maiden, the Empress of the Universe, the Eternal Bride, and he sees her in the blue sky and the heavens full of stars, as well as in the dawns and sunsets of Russia. He identifies the Beautiful Lady with a real girl, Liubov Dmitrievna Mendeleeva, whom he courts ardently in the woods and meadows of the countryside outside of Moscow, as well as in the misty maritime setting of Petersburg.

200 pages • 978-1-62138-066-5 (paper): $17.50/£11.50

www.ingramcontent.com/pod-product-compliance
Lightning Source LLC
Chambersburg PA
CBHW032017090426

42741CB00006B/635